L. BRIAN JENKINS, M.A.

KNOW MORE NONPROFITS

MOVING FROM DEPENDENCY TO SUSTAINABILITY

SUN STARTING**UP NOW**
BUSINESS SOLUTIONS

CRITICAL ACCLAIM FOR
L. BRIAN JENKINS' LATEST
KNOW MORE NONPROFITS

Know More Nonprofits is a must-read for nonprofit leaders seeking to create long-term sustainability for their organizations. Brian Jenkins has leveraged his entrepreneurism to launch, lead, and successfully attract investors to his multiple brands without becoming solely dependent upon their generosity to function.

—*Stephen H. Fraser*
Barrington Capital Partners, LLC

Know More Nonprofits is a blunt, fierce, and challenging piece that gets to the roots of the challenges of nonprofit start-ups generally and for minorities in particular. Brian makes a brilliant and compelling case for any entrepreneur or practitioner who is considering whether or not to launch his or her initiative as a nonprofit or as a for-profit enterprise. Especially powerful is his insightful and direct analysis of the impact of systemic racism on the hopes and possibilities of those who have been excluded from equal access to resources and opportunities that are generally given only to majority, largely white constituents of our economic system. He clearly details how this affects the life chances and opportunities of many today, including those who became the unwitting recipients of both de facto and de jure prejudicial favor hard wired into our American system. This is a must-read for anyone who desires to both learn and apply the principles of responsible economic reasoning that is informed by a clear social analysis of the roots of historical discrimination, even the kind endorsed by religious justification and practice.

—*Rev. Dr. Don L. Davis*
Senior Vice President, World Impact, Inc.
Executive Director, The Urban Ministry Institute

The very first paragraph of *Know More Nonprofits* compels anyone interested in nonprofit leadership to measure what they know or need to learn about the history of the nonprofit industry. Brian Jenkins expertly develops needed understanding of the industry and then truthfully reveals how the deck is stacked against minorities and women. I have personally highlighted lots of passages that I want to remember and quote to others, and I am sure you will also.

—*Dr. Zira J. Smith,*
Retired urban adult entrepreneurship educator
University of Illinois at Urbana-Champaign

For the nonprofit leaders who are committed to having lasting impact in their communities and for the men and women I know who desire to most effectively do justice in supporting them in their efforts, *Know More Nonprofits* is a value-added read. Brian Jenkins gives important context to the modern-day nonprofit world and challenges our assumptions regarding both how we got here and what must be done to create the best way forward. All may not find it a comfortable read, but I believe most will be hard-pressed to deny it is a compelling and important one.

—*Ray Carter - Executive Director*
Chicago Fellowship

Brian Jenkins is a passionate entrepreneur, teacher, and minister who has devoted his life to training and inspiring future generations of nonprofit business leaders. He boldly lives out the hard-earned truths found in this insightful and challenging book.

—*Edward Gilbreath*
Author of Reconciliation Blues and Birmingham Revolution

Printed in the United States of America

Design by Kathyjo Varco for Big Sound Music, Inc.
Photography: Sharon Hanlon
Edited by: Randi Craigen, Dawn Washington and Kyle Waalen

10 9 8 7 6 5 4 3 2 1

First Edition

- CONTENTS -

- CONTENTS -

- DEDICATION -

To My Parents

The foundation for writing *Know More Nonprofits* would be impossible without the love, support, and faithfulness of my parents, Larry and Madelyn Jenkins. Through their words, deeds, sacrifices, and ambitions for their children, they have provided the substance that *Know More Nonprofits* is built on. I will be forever thankful for their commitment to me as their son.

To My Wife

To my awesome wife of 25-years, Jenai Jenkins, whose love, support, commitment to Christ, and dedication to me and our children has provided healthy, strong, and vibrant home. Thank you for being patient with me and helping me improve each day. Your gentle spirit reminds me daily to be a better father, husband, and leader. I'm so in love in with you…

- FOREWORD -
Mark Soderquist

Brian and I first met 20 years ago when he taught an entrepreneurship class to the junior leaders in our youth program on the west side of Chicago. As a faith-based nonprofit, we recognized the importance of teaching the young leaders we were developing the value of the for-profit world. We also recognized that in our under-served urban neighborhood, there were entrepreneurs who would never get the chance to start their own business due to a lack of opportunity and capital, not a lack of intelligence or gifting. If there was any way we could open that door for them, we wanted to try. It was a joy to watch our young leaders work together to develop viable business plans and present those plans in a company boardroom.

Since then, I have worked on a number of projects with Brian as he has brought his own entrepreneurial experience and wisdom to the space between the for-profit and nonprofit worlds. We have together lamented the unjust systems still in place that place capital in the hands of people based on the color of their skin. We have spoken out against the color-coded flow of funding and resources to nonprofit organizations in the urban setting that keep white-founded and white-led organizations always at the front of the line.

What I love about Brian is that he never settles for, "This is just the way it is!" Besides speaking truth to power, he is actively trying to figure out how to make it work in the midst of unjust systems. That is where *Know More Nonprofits* comes in. Brian is making a way where there seems to be no way. As he challenges the deeply imbedded systems, he is suggesting a way around those systems instead of just waiting for change.

Some of what Brian writes may make some of us feel uncomfortable. For those of us used to privilege and power, hearing truth spoken from those who continually bump up against the unjust systems that benefit us and leave them out is seldom if ever comfortable. However if we are willing to listen redemptively, we may be allowed to participate in the next wave of entrepreneurship and nonprofit organizations that better reflect the upside-down Kingdom of God. Thank you, Brian, for pointing us in that direction!

Your partner in status quo disturbance,
Mark Soderquist

"In a sense we've come to our nation's capital to cash a check. When the architects of our republic wrote the magnificent words of the Constitution and the Declaration of Independence, they were signing a promissory note to which every American was to fall heir. This note was a promise that all men, yes, Black men as well as white men, would be guaranteed the unalienable rights of life, liberty, and the pursuit of happiness. It is obvious today that America has defaulted on this promissory note insofar as her citizens of color are concerned. Instead of honoring this sacred obligation, America has given the Negro people a bad check, a check which has come back marked insufficient funds."

"But we refuse to believe that the bank of justice is bankrupt. We refuse to believe that there are insufficient funds in the great vaults of opportunity of this nation. And so we've come to cash this check--a check that will give us upon demand the riches of freedom and the security of justice."

—Dr. Martin Luther King
Southern Christian Leadership Conference
March on Washington for Jobs and Freedom, August 28, 1963

- INTRODUCTION -
Who Should Read This Book and Why?

There are many great resources for nonprofits that are just launching. These resources include best practices for startups, traditional startup models perfected in business schools, and an overabundance of talking heads on social media and podcasts on how to get started. Believe me, I know!

I wrote *StartingUp Now: 24 Steps to Launch Your Own Business* in 2011. What is often missed, sometimes unintentionally, is the unique perspective that people of color bring to the nonprofit industry. While many nonprofits are set up to meet a societal good, the vast majority of nonprofits are not led by persons of color or women. Though their stories and strategies are unique and originate from capable, competent and experienced leaders, they often go unheard. There are a multitude of reasons why these founders' voices do not get the attention of foundations, family officers, or corporate donors. Yet they toil faithfully to fulfill their missions regardless of the absence of accolades, large donations or numerous followers on social media.

If you lack financial resources and are untrained in how the nonprofit culture works but are bold enough to try and courageous enough to fail, then *Know More Nonprofits: Moving from Dependency to Sustainability* is for you. If you are prepared to work 60-80 hours per week for years because you are filled with conviction that your idea MUST get off the ground, then *Know More* is for you. If you want to learn firsthand from mistakes made and how to recover from a free fall from someone who has made plenty of them, then *Know More* is for you. If you want to learn how the United States originated as a "startup nation," whose unique history of race, class, culture, and gender has impacted the "nonprofit industry," even in our modern era, then *Know More* is for you.

Know More is not for you if you've never failed, have never experienced frustration, or have never been tempted to say, "Forget it," and then quit! *Know More* is not for you if your privilege, power, or culture determines why your voice is heard and why you are invited to the relationship building and transformation coffees, dinners, and events and you do not see a problem with that. *Know More* is not for you if you've never had sleep-inhibited nights and lively discussions with your spouse or significant other on how bills are going to get paid while you are pursuing whatever the "it" is. If you haven't had your gas or electricity cut off because you didn't have the funds or didn't want to open the bill because you didn't have the money anyway, then *Know More* is not for you. If a faithful colleague has not lied to your face and forced legal expenses on your depleted account, then *Know More* is not for you. If you haven't had an idea snatched away, co-opted by someone who has the resources to bring it to the market but not the innovation, then *Know More* is not for you. You won't understand.

CHAPTER ONE

History Of Nonprofits

$ $ $

A nonprofit is a legal structure,
not an operational mindset.

1

Several years ago, I was speaking to the leadership of a well-known, large national/international ministry at a conference regarding entrepreneurship's direct connection to wealth creation. Based on the dialogue and interaction, it became obvious that many organizations sought to do good but had limited understanding as to why their organizations were set up as nonprofits in the first place. In fact, one person in the group was perplexed enough to honestly ask, "How can we teach others to start for-profit businesses when we have only operated as nonprofits? Why are we even set up as a nonprofit versus a for-profit?" A few years later this same person left the ministry context to pursue a Master's Degree in Economics and Public Policy at the University of Virginia.

In my book *StartingUp Now: 24 Steps to Launch Your Own Business*—a 99-page guide for people going through the business planning process for the first time—one of the most challenging chapters of the book is *Key 11: My Industry Analysis (MIA)*. This chapter requires a person to research factual information about the industry to better understand who the leaders are, changes taking place in the industry, and government regulations, along with opportunities on the horizon. Upon completing the chapter, most feel more knowledgeable and aware of the industry. In one section of the chapter I write, "It's not about becoming an industry expert, but about being able to speak *knowledgeably* about your industry."[1] The end-of-chapter reflection questions and the StartingUp Now Talks (SUN Talks) push the reader to get a better vantage point of the industry and his or her position in the industry. Upon completion, readers usually feel somewhat empowered, educated, and more aware, combating what I've termed as "industry isolation." This process helps them find out what they know and what more they need to learn, and sometimes they'll seek out

---

1 Jenkins, L. Brian. *Starting up Now: 24 Steps to Launch Your Own Business.* StartingUp Business Solutions, 2011, 34-35.

additional advice from industry experts. Researching their industry has led to organizations postponing the launch of a new product, relocation of a manufacturing facility, or even collaboration amongst competitors.

When I launched Entrenuity in 1999, I did NONE of the above and PAID dearly for it! Simply having an idea and experience was not enough. I wanted to teach entrepreneurship to urban youth so they could learn how to own their own businesses. I was attracted to entrepreneurship education because of the outcome—business skills for youth and starting businesses. I wasn't looking to get into the nonprofit industry. I was simply a person trying to do good. I knew absolutely nothing about legal structures for any type of business. I know this aspect of doing good is why many of us get involved with the nonprofit industry—but it did not excuse me from not understanding the type of industry I was involved with. I was unaware of the breadth, depth, and revenue generation of the Education and Training Services Industry (ETS) I found myself in. I had no clue that the ETS industry is comprised of 67,000 companies and generates $47 billion annually.[2] *But not knowing is not an excuse.* It was my responsibility to learn about MY INDUSTRY in order to operate more efficiently, more effectively.

> The Pew study discovered that many Americans, especially younger Americans, think religious institutions have too much power and influence on society. As those claiming any religious affiliation are declining, there will be negative economic consequences.

Simply put, a nonprofit is a legal structure, not an operational mindset. Although the nonprofit structure encompasses many types of organizations including hospitals and ministries, it also includes organizations not usually associated with being a nonprofit. The National Football League (NFL) operated as a nonprofit from its inception in 1919 until 2015 when it voluntarily relinquished its nonprofit status. There is a plethora of nonprofits in economically struggling communities. To better understand this phenomenon, it is important to understand the history of nonprofits, their role and function, and their purpose in society today.

"Education & Training Services Industry Profile." First Research, Dunn and Bradstreet, 28 Jan. 2019, www.firstresearch.com/industry-research/Education-and-Training-Services.html

For those of us in the nonprofit industry, we must dedicate ourselves to a disciplined approach in order to survive. Knowing the industry giants and influencers is paramount to our sustainability, success, and scalability. So…how did this nonprofit industry we find ourselves in get started?

Andrew Carnegie: A Giant and Influencer in Modern Philanthropy[3]

- The 1600s marked the first time nonprofits were set up in the United States. Nonprofits during this period were primarily colleges, churches, and townships that were sustained by government grants to provide public good.

- In the 1700s there was a distrust of private charities in several states. The exceptions were the states in New England that soon became the "thought leaders" in the areas of education, science, and culture.

- In the 1800s, Andrew Carnegie, a Scottish-American immigrant who became a steel tycoon, influenced many business owners to reinvest their fortunes into society. Carnegie was highly concerned with how wealth was being administered. In 1889, Carnegie's essay, *The Gospel of Wealth* addressed the issue of wealth distribution: "*The problem of our age is the proper administration of wealth, so that the ties of brotherhood may still bind together the rich and poor in harmonious relationship.*"[4] After selling Carnegie Steel Corporation to J.P. Morgan for $480 million in 1901, which would later become U.S. Steel Corporation, Carnegie devoted the remainder of his life to philanthropy, specifically giving to universities, libraries, education, and scientific research. Upon the sale of Carnegie Steel, Carnegie surpassed John D. Rockefeller as the wealthiest person in America for the next few years. Carnegie gave more than $350 million to charities and foundations and universities which would be the equivalent of $78 billion in 2015.

- Andrew Carnegie single-handedly defined philanthropical models that are still in place today. Carnegie's philanthropic practices led to the creation of many institutions that are still active today, such as Carnegie Hall, Carnegie Mellon University, and the Carnegie Corporation of New York.

- Andrew Carnegie's concern regarding wealth distribution is ever more essential today since 1% of the population controls 99% of all the wealth in the United States.

3 Andrew Carnegie, The Autobiography of Andrew Carnegie (Filiquarian Publishing, LLC, 2006).
4 Wealth by Andrew Carnegie. Edited by Robert Bannister, Swarthmore College, 1995, www.swarthmore.edu/ SocSci/rbannis1/AIH19th/Carnegie.html

- The 1900s witnessed the launch of the first foundations beginning with the Carnegie, Rockefeller, and Sage Foundation. It was during this period that fundraising became a professional industry. Volunteerism began to grow during this period, and many volunteered to lower their taxable income and impact the public good. New York, Pennsylvania, Illinois, and Ohio altered their charity statuses, leading to sweeping changes that would permit new models of philanthropy.

  o Due to the growth of charitable organizations and decreasing philanthropic dollars and donors, the community chest was formed. This led to the launch of the first "Community Organization."

  o Presidents Herbert Hoover and Franklin Delano Roosevelt believed that charitable organizations could better solve societal problems versus government programs, thereby leading to changes in the tax code and an unprecedented growth of tax-exempt charitable-based organizations.

Nonprofit Charitable Contributions – Does Not Include Religious Congregations & Organizations

Data and research (or stats) are necessary to gauge the nonprofit industry. It provides both the macro and micro views needed to better assess the potential for opportunity within the nonprofit industry, particularly for nonprofits led by non-Caucasians in the U.S. We will briefly review the variances and trends in funding nonprofits serving in the African-American and Latinx communities that are under-resourced yet led by Caucasians.

According to researcher Brice McKeever of the Urban Institute, the following data is essential to understanding the nonprofit sector as it is today: [5]

- Approximately 1.41 million nonprofits were registered with the Internal Revenue Service (IRS) in 2013, an increase of 2.8% from 2003.

- The nonprofit sector contributed an estimated $905.9 billion to the US economy in 2013, composing 5.4 percent of the country's gross domestic product (GDP).

- Of the nonprofit organizations registered with the IRS, 501(c)(3) public

---

McKeever, B. S., & Pettijohn, S. L. (2014, October). The Nonprofit Sector in Brief 2014 - Public Charities, Giving, and Volunteering. Retrieved from https://www.urban.org/sites/default/files/publication/33711/413277-The-Nonprofit-Sector-in-Brief--.PDF

charities accounted for just over three-quarters of the nonprofit sector's revenue and expenses ($1.73 trillion and $1.62 trillion, respectively) and more than three-fifths of nonprofit assets ($3.22 trillion) in 2013.

- In 2014, total private giving from individuals, foundations, and businesses totaled $358.38 billion, an increase of just over 5 percent from 2013 after adjusting for inflation. According to Giving USA (2015), total charitable giving rose for the fifth consecutive year in 2014. *After adjusting for inflation, this is the first year to exceed the previous peak set before the recession in 2007 ($355.16 billion in 2014 dollars).*

- Fully 25.3 percent of US adults volunteered with an organization in 2014, contributing an estimated 8.7 billion hours, the most hours recorded since the Current Population Survey's volunteer supplement began in 2002; the value of these hours is approximately $179.2 billion.

Based on the data provided, it is clear that the nonprofit industry has significant influence in the United States and the data above DOES NOT factor in revenue generated by Religious Congregations & Organizations (RCOs). If we factored in revenue from RCOs the amount would quadruple! Based on *The Interdisciplinary Journal of Research on Religion: The Socio-economic Contribution of Religion to American Society: An Empirical Analysis* conducted by Brian J. Grimm (Georgetown University) and Melissa Grimm (Newseum Institute), the following revenue estimates were concluded for RCOs:[6]

- Estimate #1: Revenues of faith-based organizations totaled $378 billion annually in 2016.

- Estimate #2: $1.2 trillion included the fair market value of goods and services provided by religious organizations and included contributions of businesses with religious roots.

- Estimate #3: The third, higher-end estimate of $4.8 trillion takes into account the household incomes of religiously affiliated Americans assuming that they conduct their affairs according to their religious beliefs.

Grim and Grim conclude that the second estimate of $1.2 trillion is the most reasonable because "it takes into account both the value of the services provided by religious organizations and the impact religion has on a number of important

6 Grimm, B. J., & Grimm, M. (2016). The Socio-economic Contribution of Religion to American Society: An Empirical Analysis. Retrieved from http://www.religjournal.com/

American businesses."[7] Businesses influence every facet of society. Even our religious institutions impact the nonprofit bottom line and position in American society. "Understanding the socio-economic value of religion to American society is especially important in the present era characterized by a growing disaffiliation from organized religion,"[8] the study argues, citing a recent Pew Research Center survey that found the number of religiously affiliated Americans is down to one-fifth of the population.[9] The Pew study discovered that many Americans, especially younger Americans, think religious institutions have too much power and influence on society. As those claiming any religious affiliation are declining, there will be negative economic consequences.

Given conclusive data reported by RCOs and the estimates of the Grim & Grim study, the question, "Why are we set up as a nonprofit versus a for-profit?" as asked by the person I mentioned at the beginning of this chapter, is an excellent one. As is, "Should we launch a for-profit instead of a nonprofit?" Before you can answer that question, you will need to consider and answer several others.

- CHAPTER ONE QUESTIONS -
Write your responses on page 98

1. In your community, which organizations have the most impact, nonprofits or for-profits?

2. What has been your experience with the nonprofit industry?

3. What has been your experience with the for-profit industry?

4. Which industry has produced more leaders in the United States, nonprofits or for-profits?

5. Make a list of people who personally influence you, such as mentors, people you follow on podcasts, and other influencers. Which industry have they spent the majority of their careers in, nonprofits or for-profits?

---

7 Ibid., 27.

8 Ibid., 4.

9 Smith, G. A., & Cooperman, A. (2016, September 14). The factors driving the growth of religious 'nones' in the U.S. Retrieved from https://www.pewresearch.org/fact-tank/2016/09/14/the-factors-driving-the-growth-of-religious-nones-in-the-u-s/

6. Which industry do you find more women and people of color in leadership positions, nonprofits or for-profits?

CHAPTER TWO

Why Do White Guys Have All The Money

$ $ $

"Only thank God men have done learned how to forget quick
what they ain't brave enough to try to cure."
—*The Hamlet, William Faulkner*

2

Slavery – The Foundation of America's $97 Trillion Super Power Status

As an adjunct instructor at Moody Bible Institute, I was struck by a student's question one evening while leading class. Students were at the point of identifying their sources of startup capital for the businesses they wanted to launch. One student, not from the United States and unfamiliar with America's history, asked, "Where did America get all of its wealth?" From the ensuing conversation, it was obvious that he knew very little of the history of the "American Startup Story." Over the next thirty minutes we discussed the history he was never taught—history that still is not truthfully taught in many American classrooms, churches, reservations, synagogues, and mosques. How could a startup nation of European peasants amass such wealth in such a short period of time? The answer is simultaneously simple and complicated, forced labor of Africans and intentional, systematic dehumanizing of Africans to create profits. What started as the forced labor of 19 Angolans from a Portuguese trading vessel, ultimately established America as a $97 trillion leader in the slave industry.[10] There was not one aspect of America that was untouched by the economic engine of slavery—not one! To best understand what launched America into a "thriving business" requires a thoughtful inquiry into this aspect of America's history.

> "...by 1860, there were more millionaires (slaveholders all) living in the lower Mississippi Valley than anywhere else in the United States. In the same year, the nearly 4 million American slaves were worth some $3.5 billion, making them the largest single financial asset in the entire U.S. economy..."

---

10 Blight, David. "1. Introductions: Why Does the Civil War Era Have a Hold on American Historical." YouTube, YaleCourses, 21 Nov. 2008, www.youtube.com/watch?v=QXXp1bHd6gI

Each year *Forbes Magazine* lists the wealthiest people in the world. *Forbes Magazine* typically indicates the person's name, personal net worth, business industry, size of business, and country of origin. If there were a Forbes Magazine listing of America's most wealthy business owners in 1860, all of the people listed would be slaveholders (see Reference Guide pg.114). All were immigrants. Most were Christian. Most, but not all, were men. All were Caucasian. Some inherited the "family business." Some held political office. Some were leaders in the church. All sought to expand their slave-holding empires and create even greater levels of wealth. None wanted to give up their business. This was America shortly before 1860.

According to David Blight, History Professor at Yale University, "...by 1860, there were more millionaires (slaveholders all) living in the lower Mississippi Valley than anywhere else in the United States. In the same year, the nearly 4 million American slaves were worth some $3.5 billion, making them the largest single financial asset in the entire U.S. economy, worth more than all the manufacturing and railroads combined. So, of course, the war was rooted in these two expanding and competing economies—but competing over what? What eventually tore asunder America's political culture was slavery's expansion into the Western territories." [11]

In modern dollars, $3.5 billion in 1860 equates to $97 trillion dollars! Today, the American Slave Industry of 1860 would be valued at more than the largest modern global industries of oil and gas (OPEC), retail, food and beverage, automobile and pharmaceuticals. There is simply no possible way for African Americans to reverse the effects of the intentional economic engine of assets generated by slavery without intentional economic investment. Churches and ministry leaders, specifically in the evangelical context, have almost no knowledge of the economic deprivation purposely initiated toward enslaved Black people—often with the full endorsement of southern churches. Northern U.S. and European industries benefited from the raw products of cotton—ing of the industry—to tobacco produced in the Carolinas, to the shipping industry. Cotton was manufactured with free save labor in the south, shipped to New York, and then exported to European textile industries. Slave owners often secured loans and investments by using their slaves as collateral since slaves

---

Coates, Ta-Nehisi. "What Cotton Hath Wrought." The Atlantic, Atlantic Media Company, 30 July 2010, www. theatlantic.com/personal/archive/2010/07/what-cotton-hath-wrought/60666/

were legally deemed property in the United States. When calculating the value of an estate, each slave was included as an asset (see Reference Guide pg. 115). This became the source of tax revenue for local and state governments. Taxes were also levied on slave transactions, like our modern-day sales tax. There was no way Southerners were going to give up an industry generating trillions of dollars in the U.S., Europe, Africa, the Caribbean, and South America—thus, the Civil War. Research proves how profitable this system was up and down the Afro/Euro/South American triad supply chain. It is obvious why Southerners, churches included, wanted to expand the economic engine of the slave trade. *Slavery was too profitable to give up without a major war.*

So, at this point you may be asking yourself, "How is the history of slavery in the United States relevant to my startup?" The answer is quite simple—access to capital. The majority of entrepreneurs struggle with identifying the source of the capital needed to launch their business. If you are Black, brown, or female, your struggle will be even greater. Why is this the case? Another way to ask the question stems from the late Black billionaire Reginald Lewis' bestseller, *Why Should White Guys Have All the Fun?* But for our purposes, let's ask, "Why do white guys have all the money?" Not knowing the history of the United States could reinforce the fable of "pulling yourself up by your bootstraps." Of course, that is assuming you own a pair of boots! Most African descendants of slaves, Black people, brown people, and women find themselves with very limited access to capital in the United States in 2019. This did not happen by accident. The economic condition of limiting access to capital to white male European immigrants was part of the intentional design. This design, furthered on by legislative decisions, gave preferential treatment to white males who then leveraged their preferential economic ethnic power to create businesses and industries and pass legislation intended only for the betterment and furtherance of America's European immigrants.

Businesses and individuals that provide capital opportunities for Black people, brown people, and women, help America fulfill its constitutional creed of freedom and opportunity for all its citizenry. Access to capital provides the opportunity, originally only intended for white men, to all of America's citizens. Just as the G.I. Bill provided economic opportunity for World War II veterans returning to the United States to find employment, purchase a home, get a college education, start a business, and establish themselves as part of the economic system, access to capital and wealth-building provides similar opportunities for Black people.

CHAPTER THREE

Intentional Disinvestment Warrants Intentional Investment

$ $ $

"That which is inhuman, cannot be divine."
—*Frederick Douglass*

3

I grew up in Waukegan, IL, a working-class northern suburb of Chicago. Through the recent efforts of DNA testing, my paternal side of my family can trace our lineage to the Benin/Togo areas in western Africa. Until then, my father's family was known to have migrated to Chicago via the Great Migration in the 1930's from Greenwood, Mississippi, to escape the subjugation of the Jim Crow south. It was not your traditional migration. My great Aunt Gracie Long, nee Glover, jumped on a train alone and headed to Chicago at the age of 13. She had tired of hearing her father disrespected while he sharecropped the land his grandfather had worked as a slave prior to the Civil War. As was the custom, my Aunt Gracie received her annual portion of $13.00 pay from her father and then, unbeknownst to her family, left to create a better life for herself in Chicago—a city she had heard so much about. Upon arriving on Chicago's south side, she moved in with another family from her hometown, secured a job, and began her new life. Over the next 30 years, all her siblings and her elderly mother, "Mama Glover," made the same journey from Greenwood, Mississippi to the south side of Chicago in hopes of a new life. As a youth, I distinctly remember my great grandmother's braided gray hair, leather-like hands, and the smelly Folger's coffee can containing her Garrett's tobacco spit. Mama Glover didn't speak much and, truth be told, I didn't like going into the room where she sat, since us kids would be asked to empty that smelly spit can. All these years later, I realize she was a living relic from an era which many Blacks hoped never to return…much less remember. Now I wish I could have known her—the woman, Zella Glover. What were her favorite colors, her favorite songs, her aspirations and inspirations? Was she the source of courage that emboldened my Aunt Gracie to leave Mississippi? Zella Glover was more than a field hand working on the tattered remnants of a 200-year-old plantation; she was a woman, a wife to Moses Glover for more than 50 years and the mother of 7 daughters and two sons. Zella Glover was Black and human, and her struggles and successes are a part of me.

My mother's side of the family is different. We can trace our journey through American captivity, also known as slavery, back to the Duncan Plantation in Kentucky. Through the tremendous efforts of my cousin, Renee Howard, we know the Duncans immigrated from Scotland around 1799, got off the ship with almost no savings, and quickly joined the most lucrative industry in America—an industry sanctioned and endorsed by the church, protected by the state, and encouraged by most. My great grandfather, Leonard Q. Duncan, was born into a challenging family situation near Cave in Rock, IL. Leonard was sent "away" to be raised by a white family who treated him fairly, educated him as best they could, and provided an environment that was healthy until he could earn his keep. He was 10 years old. The white family was actually his paternal side of the family. *You see, my great grandfather's father, the Scottish Harvey Duncan, often visited the slave quarters of his plantation.* My great grandfather Leonard, and his brother Karl, were just two of the "mulatto" children sired by Harvey and other Duncan family members. Leonard eventually married Mildred "Minnie" Duncan, a woman with a fiery personality and, according to family stories, a "good shot" who was known to protect her own. My grandmother, Ressie Mae Duncan, was the second of nine children born to their union. Ressie, "Grandma," eventually married Joseph "Grandad" Thomas, my maternal grandfather, who had been raised as an orphan in foster care. Grandad was a hired hand on the farm owned by my Grandpa Duncan and took an immediate interest in my grandmother. Their courtship was short, and they married within six months of meeting each other at the ages of 18 and 20 years old, just before my grandfather was drafted into World War II. To their union five children were born, including my mother, Madelyn Jenkins, nee Thomas.

Prior to relocating to North Chicago in 1959 in search of better jobs, my grandfather worked in the coal mines near Carrier Mills. During these times, Black men often worked in the most dangerous, deepest part of the mines, with the least amount of respiratory protection, for less than half the pay white men received. However, as many Black men of that era did each day, my grandfather did whatever was necessary to provide for his family. That mine killed my grandfather. On July 29, 1982, when I was just 16, I watched my grandfather

> **There is not one aspect of America that has not been touched or has not benefited from Black labor. Not one.**

lose his battle with Black Lung Disease as he gasped to breathe. He was only 64 years old. That experience left a memorable impression on me. I enjoyed learning to fish and hunt with him. I wish I could have known him, not just as Grandad, but as the man, Joseph Thomas. By all accounts, he ALWAYS provided for his family, often letting his children eat first after working 13-hour days. My mother still remarks to this day that, "Daddy always let us eat first, and we never went hungry."

Understanding why investment is needed for African Americans directly impacted by slavery often requires a personal relational experience. My family's story is not unique. My family's experience of overcoming when EVERYTHING was stacked against them is the American experience of many Blacks. Except for a few fiercely brave, white abolitionists, Blacks had almost no one contending for their well-being. There was no investment. There was only intentional disinvestment—legislatively, educationally, economically, and politically. Terrorism against Blacks through the lynching of Black men, the raping of adolescent Black girls, and the theft of Black-owned land, forced many Blacks to live in isolation from Caucasians. This is the America that my family survived, while still being fundamentally loyal in hope that America would one day recognize their humanity, their dignity, and their contribution. Their desire was to simply be a part of the "Promise of America" that Caucasians got to enjoy—a promise that benefited from Black labor in every tenet. *There is not one aspect of America that has not been touched or has not benefited from Black labor. Not one.*

Black Americans today have been directly impacted by 400 years of slavery, Jim Crow laws that inhibited Black progress from the 1870's–1960's, legislative laws [1] passed by the U.S. Supreme Court intent on disinvestment, and unprecedented mass incarceration. Just as the waves of a large ship slams the shore, raising some boats and capsizing others, America has an obligation to invest in its Black citizens directly impacted by its history. America must intentionally invest in Black lives. They do matter. The key areas of investment should be known and evident:

- Black Humanity
- Black Male Personhood

---

12 "List of Landmark African-American Legislation." Wikipedia, Wikimedia Foundation, 4 Apr. 2019, en.wikipedia.org/wiki/List_of_landmark_African-American_legislation

- Black Womanhood
- Black Economic Opportunity
- Black Legislation
- Black Educational Opportunities

Black People Are Fully Human – The Three Fifths Compromise in 1787, a decision between northern and southern states, determined that Black slaves only counted as 3/5 of a person. This decision was effective in determining how many representatives the free whites should have in the House of Representatives. Hence the name "3/5 Compromise."

Black Male Personhood – Black men must be recognized as men. White America's longstanding efforts to construct Black men into their own invented caricatures speaks to white America's own fears and phobias. If you can control the image, you can control the narrative. From the very first advertisements for slave auctions in Jamestown, VA, to the modern-day media-fixation and depiction of the powerful conquering Black athlete, stereotypes of the Black man have dominated American society at every level.

Black Womanhood – From the pleas of a slave named Angela, who passionately sought to persuade her captors to free her after the ship carrying her docked at Plymouth Rock in 1619, since she was "a Christian just like them," to the immortal words of Sojourner Truth spoken at the Women's Convention in 1851, *"Ain't I a Woman,"* Black women have struggled for recognition regarding their humanity and gender equality. Black womanhood is unique and must be treasured. Black womanhood built America by sacrificing their visions for themselves in hopes of better futures for their families. Where I'm from in Waukegan/North Chicago, IL, it was common for Black women to "work down the line" providing cleaning and childcare services to white families in affluent communities such as Lake Forest, Glencoe, Highland Park and others. The line was literally the railroad line that connected northern suburban communities to Chicago. Many Black women would often "go down line" and work 12-hour days taking care of white children and then go home to take care of their own families. Black women have traditionally worked outside the home, taking care of white families and then taking care of their own.

Black women have also withstood sexual assault without the protection of legislation. During the recent Supreme Court hearing of Justice Brett Kavanaugh in September 2018, the sexual harassment and sexual assault that many women have withstood was front and center as Dr. Christine Blasey-Ford recounted her experience of being assaulted by Brett Kavanaugh at a party in the early 1980s. The illegal assault Dr. Blasey-Ford experienced is the similar assault tens of thousands of Black girls, teenagers, and women were subjected to on every step of their journey to America. It was a well-known practice on slave ships to have women chained together when brought to the deck of the ships. This was to lessen the likelihood that women would throw themselves overboard rather than endure the repeated sexual assaults and sanctioned rapes by the crewmen during the Middle Passage. Rather than be raped repeatedly, thousands threw themselves overboard to be eaten alive by sharks or to drown in the ocean. Hugh Thomas, author of *The Slave Trade: The Story of the Atlantic Slave Trade, 1440-1870*,[13] conservatively estimates that as many as 1.2–2.5 million predominantly West Africans died during the Transatlantic Middle Passage from the 16th to 19th century. Black women have endured more than any other women in America but still remain resilient and strong and represent a pillar in the African-American diaspora. Black women must be treasured, held in esteem, and never subjected to being treated as less than human. Never again.

Black Economic Opportunity After Emancipation – By all accounts lack of economic opportunity was the first and foremost obstacle to my family's survival in America. America's history clearly informs us that America had no intention of seeing its Black citizens as part of the majority citizenry, much less to prosper economically. Almost every law was intent on castigating its Black citizens to an inferior status. It is almost entirely impossible to gain an economic foothold, when one is not recognized as being human. It was not until the 14th Amendment of the U.S. Constitution in 1868[14] that African Americans were recognized as full citizens. Another 100 years of Jim Crow Laws sanctioning terrorism often with the support and direct involvement of law enforcement

---

13 Thomas, Hugh, The Slave Trade: The Story of the Atlantic Slave Trade, 1440-1870 (New York: Simon & Schuster, 1999).

14 "U.S. Constitution - Amendment 14 - The U.S. Constitution Online." Amendment 14 - The U.S. Constitution Online - USConstitution.net, www.usconstitution.net/xconst_Am14.html

officers, ultimately led to the rise of the young preacher, Martin King, to lead the Civil Rights Movement. After being at the forefront of the Civil Rights Movement for almost 15 years, King, from a middle-class Black family himself, saw the next mountain to cross: battling for economic opportunity for African Americans. In his last book ever written, *Where Do We Go From Here: Chaos or Community*, King knew that African-American progress was dependent on economic opportunity.[15] Without establishing an economic foothold, the gains and goals of the Civil Rights Movement would be difficult to fulfill.

Black Legislation – To combat the 400 years of free labor through slavery, there needs to be intentional legislation to repair Black humanity and economic capacity. When Zacchaeus, a swindler and a cheat, was visited by Jesus, his repentance—marked by intentionality—was commended. Zacchaeus chose to repay four times what he had stolen to those he intentionally cheated and wronged and Jesus said, "Today, salvation has come to this house."[16] What if America had policies and provisions to restore at the bare minimum four times what America earned from its African-American captives? What might that look like for African Americans if that practice had been followed at the end of the Civil War? In fact, we would only be in the 153rd year of the economic repair at the time of this writing! In his book, *Being Black, Living in the Red: Race, Wealth, and Social Policy in America*, noted sociologist Dalton Conley's research finds that when all factors are equal, regardless of race, problems that plague poor communities almost completely disappear.[17] America, with a closed fist, dished out 400 years of legislation intent on destabilizing every aspect of Black life. What would 400 years of legislation, with an open hand, intent on righting that wrong look like? Legislation matters!

> Dependency on funding from others to solve problems creates a culture of cannibalism versus a culture of commerce.

---

15 Martin Luther King, Jr. Where Do We Go from Here: Chaos or Community? (Boston, MA: Beacon Press, 2010).

16 "Luke 19, New International Version (NIV) | The Bible App." Holy Bible, YouVersion, 1996, www.bible.com/bible/111/LUK.19.NIV

17 Dalton Conley, Being Black, Living in the Red: Race, Wealth, and Social Policy in America (Berkley & Los Angeles, CA: University of California Press, 1999, 2019).

Black Educational Opportunities – The *Brown vs. Topeka Board of Education*[18] decision, one of the catalyst decisions of the Civil Rights Movement in 1954, ended the practice that allowed state laws that established the constitutionality of separate public schools for Black and white students. This Supreme Court decision was in direct contrast to the *Plessy vs. Ferguson*[19] decision in 1896, that established the "separate but equal" status only 58 years earlier. The separation of Black and white students with unequal access to educational funding, unequal access to schools, unequal access to the number of teachers in a classroom, unequal access to the locations of schools, was not fully dismantled, but one of Caucasians' last bastions of "separate but equal" was legislatively undone—at least in principle. Harmful educational policies, intent on providing inferior and unequal resources to its Black citizenry, requires educational policies intent on repairing the generational wrongs of these policies. I would be remiss if I failed to mention that in direct contrast to the *Plessy vs. Ferguson* decision of 1896, this period saw the rapid rise of more than 100 Historically Black Colleges and Universities (HBCUs). HBCUs often provided the only opportunities for Black men and women to receive education in safe, culturally conducive environments intent on molding leaders to compete at all levels of American society. Education is one of the pillars of almost every ethnic group seeking to gain a better foothold in America. Just as the Federal G.I. Bill afforded Caucasian soldiers returning from World War II subsidized educational opportunities which in turn helped create the middle class, African Americans have always viewed education as one of the pillars for Black progress in the United States. With the success of the Civil Rights Movement to eventually remove federal and state legislated race-based educational roadblocks, at least in theory, African Americans would now receive intentional educational investment, again in theory. However, more than six decades later, a significant gap still exists between the funding of educational resources for African-American students and Caucasian students. In a recent study, "Funding Gaps: An Analysis of School Funding Equity Across the U.S. and Within Each State," the Education Trust found the funding gaps between wealthy students and students in high poverty districts to be staggering.

---

18 "Brown v. Board of Education (1954)." Our Documents - Brown v. Board of Education (1954), www.ourdocuments.gov/doc.php?flash=false&doc=87#

19 "Plessy v. Ferguson (1896)." Our Documents - Plessy v. Ferguson (1896), www.ourdocuments.gov/doc.php?flash=false&doc=52

Of course, it is my State of Illinois that was of particular significance. In Illinois, students in areas deemed as high poverty received 22% less in educational resources in comparison to students from non-high-poverty areas. Illinois and other states with high concentrations of impoverished students must be intentional in education to counter the known chasm and the limited opportunities unequal education opportunities create.[20]

So, what does all of this mean? What does this have to do with nonprofits or for-profits? Doing good in Black communities requires intentional investment in the six areas mentioned above: Black Humanity, Black Male Personhood, Black Womanhood, Black Economic Opportunity, Black Legislation, and Black Educational Opportunities. Black Americans seeking to create generational economic opportunity MUST focus on business creation and development. Dependency on grants funded by taxpayers limits and restricts entrepreneurial creativity. Dependency on funding from others to solve problems creates a culture of cannibalism versus a culture of commerce. Relying only on donor generosity to do good in a community does not generate sustainability or independence. While funding from Religious Congregations & Organizations (RCOs) has been a hallmark for American culture, particularly the mighty Black Church, now required are new funding sources not bound by parishioners passing the plate. Due to the steady decline in the number of Americans even associating themselves with a religious organization, this source of funding is increasingly becoming unreliable and nonexistent. The sustainability of healthy Black communities cannot be dependent upon nonprofits or religious organizations but is directly linked to business development.

- CHAPTER THREE QUESTIONS -

Write your responses on page 100

1. Has your organization experienced disinvestment or do you work in a community that has experienced generational or historical disinvestment?

Amerikaner, Ary. "Funding Gaps 2018." The Education Trust, edtrust.org/resource/funding-gaps-2018/

2. How has your organization benefited from America's intentional disinvestment of Black people?

3. How has your organization performed intentional investment with its time, talent, influence and financial resources? What are the measurable impacts that can be reported on your organization's investment?

4. Of the intentional investment activities led by your organization, which are scalable and replicable?

5. How has your organization acknowledged and/or contributed to Black Humanity?

6. How has your organization acknowledged and/or contributed to Black Male Personhood?

7. How has your organization acknowledged and/or contributed to Black Womanhood?

8. How has your organization acknowledged and/or contributed to Black Economic Opportunity?

9. How has your organization acknowledged and/or contributed to Black Legislation?

10. How has your organization acknowledged and/or contributed to Black Educational Opportunities?

CHAPTER FOUR

White Evangelical Economic Privilege (WEEP)

$ $ $

"The scandal of the evangelical mind is that there is not much of an evangelical mind."
—*Mark A. Knoll,*
The Scandal of the Evangelical Mind

4

Prior to launching Entrenuity and while job hunting, I was recruited by several nondenominational ministries. With my black face, Wheaton College credentials, young family, and supportive wife, I was a rare find. A large organization that will remain "Anonymous" was very interested in securing us as a couple. I was in dialogue with Anonymous for several weeks, and Anonymous encouraged me to launch Entrenuity as part of their organization. Essentially, I would be the director, but Anonymous would be the owner. They would supply me with the capital and much of the infrastructure I desperately needed, such as a salary for my young family. To say this was attractive is an understatement! There were aspects to the opportunity that attracted me—the commitment to an urban context, the commitment to youth and training leaders, along with being part of a larger, well-established organization with financial resources. However, upon further dialogue and learning that Anonymous was essentially giving me an advance on a salary I would eventually have to repay, along with replacing the funds for the ministry, via support raising, it became quite clear that my freedom would be handily restricted and I would retain no ownership myself! Our negotiations eventually came to an impasse as it became obvious Anonymous wanted to control not only my support raising through the "starter relationships," but they would also own my ideas, my concepts, and my dreams. Their proposed process devalued my freedom and legally bound me to their direction, since I would only be a director, not a founder with equity.

Problem:
In the Evangelical Urban Ministry Industry, the leaders with direct relationships to financial decision makers in corporations, foundations, and with private individuals for fundraising are almost always Caucasian. In many cases, the leadership is not of the same ethnicity as those they seek to minister to. The executive directors and presidents are most often Caucasian and so the ministries with direct connections to funding sources are consistently Caucasian

led. Urban ministries that are led by indigenous ethnic minority leadership, particularly African-American and Latinx, often lack direct access to financial decision makers. Therefore, the standard funding model within the Evangelical Urban Ministry Industry is problematic for minority-led organizations.

I have personally experienced several challenges with this model over the years. These challenges include a lack of understanding of the historical and legislated denial of African-American participation in the free market system. Some challenges have manifested themselves through a lack of cultural respect and dignity for those being served. The psychosis of racism, as it relates to funding within the evangelical community, as well as within our ministries and churches is less obvious to identify. Many of my African-American and Latinx colleagues, along with a handful of Asian brothers, have lamented about how debilitating the existing deputation system can be.

Evangelical Urban Ministry "Industry" Analysis

A cursory overview of the Evangelical Urban Ministry Industry finds the existing deputation system is problematic for ethnic minorities and effective for Caucasian led ministries:

- Ministries led by African Americans and Latinx leaders do not have access to secure capital from private donors, foundations, and corporations.

- Ministries led by African Americans and Latinx leaders are disproportionately under-capitalized while tasked with the greatest sense of responsibility for their own communities.

- Almost 92% of evangelical donors give to Caucasian-led, non-indigenous urban ministries in Chicago.

- Ministries led by African Americans and Latinx leaders often do not have the operational infrastructure, support networks, experienced leadership, and Board of Directors for long-term ministry effectiveness.

According to a survey of 16 urban ministries in Chicago, based on their 2012-2013 IRS 990s and detailed in the charts below, the following observations were made:

- White-led organizations raised $35 million compared to $1.7 million raised by African-American and Latinx-led organizations, accounting for 96% of the income raised that year.

- White, female-led organizations raised 78% of the total income in 2012-2013, even though they represented only 25% of the organizations surveyed.

- White-led urban ministries secured higher levels of funding overall, leading to sustained ministry presence overall, regardless of their relevance or impact in the community.

- White-led urban ministries had access to significantly higher levels of funding in shorter time periods and in spite of less proven experience in the field.

- White ministry leaders averaged more business related degrees while African-American and Latinx ministry leaders had degrees in religious related studies, which directly impacted fundraising.

- White ministry leaders from outside the community raised significantly higher levels of funding than indigenous, grassroots leaders.

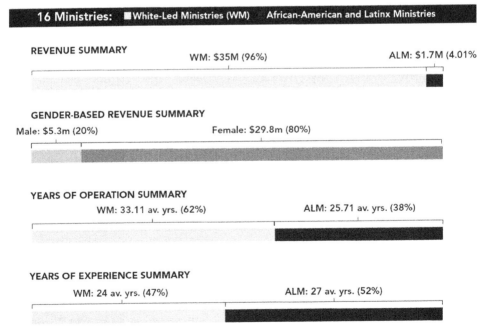

Evangelical Urban Ministries in Chicago: Summary
Charts below represent data from urban ministries only (not churches) based on their individual 2012-2013 IRS 990 filing.

16 Ministries: ■White-Led Ministries (WM)　African-American and Latinx Ministries

REVENUE SUMMARY
WM: $35M (96%)　　　　ALM: $1.7M (4.01%

GENDER-BASED REVENUE SUMMARY
Male: $5.3m (20%)　　　Female: $29.8m (80%)

YEARS OF OPERATION SUMMARY
WM: 33.11 av. yrs. (62%)　　　ALM: 25.71 av. yrs. (38%)

YEARS OF EXPERIENCE SUMMARY
WM: 24 av. yrs. (47%)　　　ALM: 27 av. yrs. (52%)

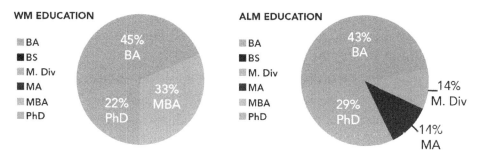

See Reference Guide, pgs. 116-123 for a more in-depth look at the above summary or download at startingupnow.com/KMNP_charts.pdf

Evangelical Urban Ministry Cultural Challenges

While many evangelical urban ministries with Caucasian leadership often have great intent, their models are based upon their own cultural values and norms. Being fully conscious and accepting of a person's culture is KEY for lasting impact. Some of the cultural challenges that exist in traditional Caucasian-led urban ministries are:

- Many ministries set up and launch within a community without being invited, without respecting and sometimes even acknowledging the pastors, churches and ministries that have served in the community for decades.

- Many non-indigenous, Caucasian, urban ministry leaders are celebrated as heroes and heroines in Caucasian churches, schools, and organizations. They are often requested to speak about the great "work" they are doing and to tell the story to white people of how they "moved" into a challenging community.

- Many non-indigenous, Caucasian-led ministries position the organization or leader to be in command/control with almost no intent for those being served to ultimately be in leadership.

- Many non-indigenous, Caucasian-led urban ministries' marketing/funding models are emotive-based and reinforce negative stereotypes already held by their financial supporters.

- Many non-indigenous, Caucasian-led, urban ministries' funding mechanisms (dinners, events, socials) are based on the ministry leader being the primary connector to donors, without facilitating a relationship between those that fund the ministry and the indigenous ministry leaders.

- Many non-indigenous, Caucasian-led urban ministries target a community with an entry plan but without an exit strategy—there is almost never a plan to leave and transfer funding, relationships, networks, and power to the indigenous leaders in the communities served.

Solution:

To solve the problem, a paradigm shift is needed—a paradigm that at its very core, begins and ends with equally valuing all people with dignity and respect. This allows for a level of trust to emerge that is based on peer-to-peer relationships where people are valued as colleagues—not just the recipients of benevolence. By intentionally serving others with excellence and dignity, we value their humanness

> Being Black and human forces America to rethink and reimagine its promise to ALL of its citizens.

and establish a sense of expectation. We provide our best resources with the expectation that they will be used purposely for the goals and objectives of the church, ministry or organization. *We train for success. We train expecting results*

This shift is similar to Dr. Don Davis' Principal of Reversal (see Reference Guide pgs. 116-123) within the context of Scripture. The Principal of Reversal follow Jesus' model in which the poor, the disenfranchised, and those on the margin of society ultimately become the founders of the Christian church. In the sam way, the indigenous persons in the communities we serve should become th leaders and decision makers in their churches and ministries. The indigenou leaders of churches and ministries should be trained and ultimately positione to have a direct relationship with CEOs, sponsors, and private funders rathe than a filtered third- or fourth-tiered relationship simply as a recipient c generosity. There must be an intentional inclusionary effort to train, resourc and equip indigenous ethnic leaders to serve indigenous ethnic persons in their own communities. This will require minimum input from those non-ethnic, non-indigenous leaders, often Caucasian, who have come from outside of the community to minister to African-American and Latinx communities. The indigenous leaders should ultimately have first-tier relationships with those who seek to provide financial resources to assist their ministry efforts. Possible solution-based goals are:

1. Unlock access to potential investors via ministry pitch events.
2. Connect urban churches/ministries with mentors.
3. Prepare urban churches/ministries to receive funding.
4. Launch an urban church/ministry accelerator that creates a culture of innovative approaches to solving urban challenges.
5. Guide an urban ministry/church through the process of launching a business, social enterprise or ministry.

There are many urban ministries and churches that have never had an opportunity to share their vision, values, and commitment to their communities with potential funders due to the existing fundraising paradigms utilized by majority culture ministries.

I believe it should be stated upfront that there will be risks and rewards, but I believe a new paradigm can serve as a resource for multiple urban outposts for Christ and provide a sustainable model that can be replicated.

Back to the Anonymous Ministry and what might have been: Let's do a revisionist's history of what could have happened if I worked with them. If the Anonymous Ministry decided to invest early in the idea of Entrenuity versus adopting a posture of owning and controlling the idea, the following events might have occurred in real-time:

- Entrenuity launches in 1999 with full-funding and staff infrastructure in place and immediately begins making an impact on youth and youth leaders in after-school programs;
- Entrenuity is able to secure funding to secure Duane Moyer, longtime colleague and friend to focus on operations and growth while Jenkins focuses on teacher and student development tools and resources;

- Entrenuity's use of Moyer's curriculum, *Creating True Wealth*, is published by Anonymous Ministry and is used by Anonymous' sites both nationally and globally to introduce entrepreneurship to churches and ministries;

- Entrenuity launches its first Entrenuity Summer Business Camp in the Summer of 2000, hosting more than 250 African-American and Latinx students along with introducing more than 3,000 students and their families to Wheaton College due to recruitment efforts;

- Entrenuity students extraordinaire, Stephan Hall and Delano Taylor, are featured in the PBS documentary, *These Kids Mean Business*, having launched D & S Snacks Catering and generated $30,000 as 8th grade students at Roseland Christian School. Hall and Taylor provide a large donation, saving the school from closing due to lack of funding for a 50-year-old Christian school in the predominantly African-American community of Roseland on Chicago's south side;

- In the midst of the recession, Entrenuity launches *StartingUp Now: 24 Steps to Launch Your Own Business* with the full resources and support of Anonymous Ministry, thereby expanding the number of youth impacted by the Gospel of Entrepreneurship in churches/ministries to more than 100,000 in multiple languages;

- In addition, Entrenuity launches the StartingUp Now Skillcenter, a cloud-based business planning platform with support services for growth;

- Skillcenter allows Entrenuity to effectively train both the youth and their parents/families with the Gospel of Entrepreneurship;

- *StartingUp Now* sells over 100,000 books and Skillcenter has over 10,000 users, both youth and adult, at a global level;

- Entrenuity launches Moxe, a co-sharing space for urban youth to connect with like-minded youth to grow their business from;

- Entrenuity launches the Duncan Legacy Fund with $500,000 to loan startup capital to youth and adult entrepreneurs;

- Entrenuity's successful selection and investment model leads to the launch of the Moxe Impact Fund, an impact investment fund focused on investments into Black- and Latinx- owned businesses.

While I certainly am thankful and grateful for the challenges that I overcame from 1999-2019 in launching Entrenuity, reflecting on what might have been is both painful and eye-opening. The challenges I had to overcome beginning in 1999 have improved, but there is much progress that still needs to occur in 2019. Yes, there have been great friends and relationships made over the past 20 years, but I'm wondering how much being a Black-led organization has stifled Entrenuity's progress.

I state with conviction that if I had launched Entrenuity as a white-male or a white-female, the funding opportunities would have been immediate. As a result, my education credentials would not have been questioned. My Black, middle class upbringing, being raised by parents who have been married for more than 50 years and sacrificially provided a stable, supportive environment, would be viewed as an asset, not an anomaly. My ability to speak with articulation, to correctly conjugate verbs, and my creativity and confidence would not be viewed as arrogant, but as assurance in knowing WHO I am. The originality of Entrenuity and my authorship of *StartingUp Now*, StartingUp Now Skillcenter, SUN Talks, and the launch of Moxe would not be called into question. Unfortunately, these are the challenges many who look like me, especially Black men, are conditioned to deal with.

Being Black, male, and human in the United States should be celebrated, not perceived as a threat. Being Black and human in the United States epitomizes and defines resiliency. Being Black and human is an American tragedy still being played on stage. America's least celebrated citizenry, brought intentionally and disavowed after emancipation, now defines hope amidst chaos. Being Black and human forces America to rethink and re-imagine its promise to ALL of its citizens. Black citizen contributions have propelled America to its superpower status. America has a debt that must be repaid to its Black citizens that will take generations to balance the scales.

CHAPTER FIVE

Social Enterprise Vs. Business Ownership
Which is better for economically challenged communities?

$ $ $
"Always know the difference between
what you're getting and what you deserve."
—*Reginald Lewis*
Founder and CEO, TLC Group Beatrice

5

A few years ago, I polled friends representing various professions, ages, genders, education levels, and locations throughout the United States with the following question: "Does the Black community in the United States need social enterprises or traditional businesses?" The majority agreed the need was for traditional businesses. An obvious follow up question I asked was, "What is the reason for your decision?" The reasons varied, based on the person's experience, occupation, and situation in life, but all agreed on one reason: wealth creation. *The ability to create wealth or pass down wealth is the common denominator to communities becoming economically stable.* This principle became immediately apparent when I first entered the nonprofit industry to work at an urban ministry early in my career. I quickly discovered that the very principles that helped majority Caucasian/white-led ministries raise money impeded wealth creation for Black and brown people. One such principle consisted of living in the target community to "better understand" the ministry environment.

Relocation Gone Wrong
Purchasing Homes in Austin vs. Oak Park, IL – Housing Value

For many Americans, owning a home is the greatest asset they will purchase in their lifetime and pass down to their children. In 1996, my wife and I were earnestly seeking to purchase our first home. Our commitment of serving in the urban context, living in the community, working in the community, and raising our family in the community limited our search to only urban communities on Chicago's West Side. We also had friends of a similar background with the same commitment to serve in the urban context but who wanted to purchase a home in Oak Park, a suburb adjacent to Chicago. Oak Park is known for its world famous Frank Lloyd Wright homes, commitment to diversity, good schools, and general overall charm. While both communities appealed to us, we ended up purchasing in the Austin community versus Oak Park in 1997 purely for the commitment of living in the urban context. In fact, the ministry my wife worked for at the time required its entire staff to live in the community.

As a young couple purchasing our first home, we were not "encouraged" to consider the financial implications of purchasing our home in an economically distressed community. We were only focused on living in the community among the people we served. Therefore, we purchased our home in 1997 for $95,000. Another couple, lifelong friends of ours, purchased their home in Oak Park in the same year for $157,000—quite a significant difference in pricing. The stark difference in our investments became immediately obvious as our friends had access to better school choices, healthier food options, fewer potholes on their streets, safety for their children, and a beautiful downtown shopping area. Over the next 20 years, their home appreciated in value from their original purchase price of $157,000 to $425,000. The increased value of more than $268,000 allowed them to survive a loss of a job, avert a minor health crisis, purchase an investment property, save money for their children's college education, and provide loans for their children for various economic needs.

In contrast, the value of our home only increased from $95,000 to $215,000 over the same 20-year period—an increase of $120,000. While we are thankful for an increase in the value of our home, there is a vast difference in the equity. As urban dwellers, we quickly learned how to navigate the Chicago Public School's elementary and high school selective enrollment process. We learned how to create opportunities for our children by setting high expectations for them regardless of their zip code. We provided our children with opportunities outside of the school system for sports, the arts, camps and cross-country vacations. We have been blessed with our children and are extremely proud of their character, academic performance, and resiliency. We are looking forward to seeing them develop into the people God has designed them to be as they pursue the path He has for each of them. Over these last 25 years, we have been exceedingly blessed and are thankful for the circumstances, challenges, and opportunities we have experienced by living in the Austin community. However, the variance in equity still exists.

While we are committed to the work of urban ministry, the unspoken and spoken badge of honor was living in the "hood," which gave credibility...if you were white! But we are Black. We couldn't market our ministerial reasons for purchasing a home in Austin in the same way a white couple could market purchasing a home and raising their family in the inner city.

Black People Ministering to Black People DOES NOT SELL to White People

Although I never considered using our story and status to raise our ministry profile or our funding, it became obvious that many white-led ministries touted in their marketing materials how their staff lived in chaotic, gang-filled communities. We did not have a donor base to market our decision to do the same. Black people moving into a Black community to minister among other Black people...that doesn't sell! In fact, we spent more time explaining why we were partnering with a white ministry instead of becoming ministers in a Black church. My wife's uncle, founder of a large prominent Missionary Baptist Church in Cleveland, would often remark that he was focused on "people development, not community development."

Mission Organizations vs. Traditional Church

The traditional Black church in America financially supports church-based ministry, not necessarily parachurch organizations. Many of my friends and colleagues adopted fundraising principles successfully practiced by white-led ministries functioning in Black/brown communities. However, many Black/brown people with high hopes for ministry have led their families into financial chaos trying to launch a ministry with models that have proven culturally unconducive. While sacrifice is often required in launching anything, it is much more challenging when you are encouraged and required to use models that simply do not work. Pursuing these models and methods have led to a person's commitment, work ethic and personal integrity being questioned. The sacrifices being made are often at the expense of the person's quality of his or her marriage, being both present and involved with their children's lives and activities, along with the mental anguish of not succeeding regardless of the tremendous amount of effort being made. Models that are not meant for you are simply not meant for you. They must be abandoned without inflicting damage to the person and his or her family that only years of professional counseling may be able to heal. This is the plight of many African-American ministry leaders often in Caucasian-led, nonprofit ministry structures.

If you were Black or Brown, the question from many was, "Why live in an economically disadvantaged neighborhood in the city, instead of a suburb like Oak Park?" To be honest, that question plagued me for the next 20 years and still does today.

White-led ministries often market the "missionary families," who move into the community and live among the people they serve, in their fundraising marketing materials, individual support letters, and annual events. Their marketing tactics often serve to reinforce the over-hyped negative stereotype many white people already have of the city. One ministry I know created a video of youth from the ministry roasting marshmallows around a campfire in an alley—something I've never seen before! While the youth are roasting the marshmallows, gunfire erupts and the youth scatter. A white youth worker from the ministry then appears, gathers the youth back, consoles them, and then the ministry's logo and contact information appear on the screen requesting donations for the ministry! When I first saw this, I was horrified that a ministry would exploit youth in such a way! I recall thinking, *my parents would NEVER allow me or my sister to be pimped for profits and media impressions.* However, I soon learned this level of intentional exploitation, under the guise of "doing good," was a standard operating procedure for many ministries in the "urban market." Ironically, I got to know each of the youth in the video. As adults, they now realize the exploitative nature of that marketing. They each have a distant relationship with the ministry and would NEVER allow their own children to be exploited. The very people born and raised in the community are not afforded the option to raise financial support and write letters to a donor base to fund where they live and minister. Yet they are encouraged to remain in the community by the very people whose relocation gives them an economic advantage.

> It's not always about who can be the most effective at ministry, but it's often about who can raise the most money.

The practice of relocating is not new, as Dr. Martin Luther King relocated to the North Lawndale Community on the West Side of Chicago in 1966 to better understand the economic despair and racial challenges experienced by the many Blacks who migrated there to escape the Jim Crow south during the Great Migration. King had grown up in Atlanta in a Black middle-class family with the means to provide young Martin with educational opportunities and other amenities. From what King experienced during the summer of 1966, he remarked that the racism in the North was at a different level than the racism he had grown up with in the South.[21]

---

21 "I have never seen, even in Mississippi and Alabama, mobs as hateful as I've seen here in Chicago," Dr. Martin Luther King, Jr. MyFootage001. "Dr. King - Housing March in Gage Park Chicago, 1966." YouTube, 18 Oct. 2007, www.youtube.com/watch?v=r_pjbnMXM1o

When I first told my dad about the ministry I was involved with and the requirement to live in the community, he asked, "Where does the president of the ministry live?" When I told him the president/founder of the ministry lived in the suburbs and not in the community as required of the staff, my dad said, "What in the hell kind of game is he playing? Requiring you to live in the city while he and his family live in the suburbs? That's some bull----!" This is the type of blue-collar common sense I was privileged to grow up with in the home of Larry and Madelyn Jenkins. Their no nonsense, straight-to-the-point, working-class wisdom led to them creating an economic base that provided me with a very stable upbringing and financial help at various times. Trying to explain why I wanted to be part of an organization that required ministry staff to "raise support" or in my dad's words, "beg for money," was so culturally isolated, it made no sense. In the church where I grew up, First Corinthian Missionary Baptist Church in North Chicago, IL, even the founding pastor worked! When my dad found out the president of the ministry received a salary, health care benefits, a retirement plan, and a percentage of each dollar raised by ministry staff, the language became much more colorful! The model might work when raising money from a predominantly Caucasian funding base, but if your funding base was Black, blue-collar workers with common sense, it was downright debilitating, and oftentimes humiliating. Although I made several lifelong friends and colleagues at this ministry, the model was not scalable. It was only transferable to those within the Caucasian ministry culture and certainly not replicable in comparison to launching a business. Caucasian ministries that primarily use Caucasian ministry principles to financially support their efforts, such as fundraising, by default keep the ministry staff and administration just that—primarily Caucasian. *It's not always about who can be the most effective at ministry, but it's often about who can raise the most money. It's often about who can best assimilate into Caucasian ministry practices and culture, not who is best equipped for ministry within their own culture and environment.*

What if ministries focused on creating business ownership models for those they serve within the context of ministry? What if the ministries intentionally transferred relationships to potential leaders from the community with a clearly planned exit strategy? What if urban ministry leaders provided startup capital for businesses launched by those trained in the community so they could make their own decisions? What if ministry leaders involved the already existing leadership in the communities versus completely overlooking their longstanding leadership? Business ownership is power. Non-owners are dependent on those that broker the relationships. Business owners have decision-making capacity.

Non-owners live with others' decisions, often made outside the community, that are not always in their best interest but in the best interest of the ministry itself. Business owners can legally transfer ownership of a business to family members. Non-owners transfer nothing. In fact, non-owners are not provided the opportunity to broker the relationships. Their relationships are typically with, you guessed it, other non-owners!

Therefore, trying to understand why launching social enterprises in communities that are struggling economically might raise similar questions and levels of consternation. Most urban ministries I'm connected with in Chicago rarely teach or integrate economic principles, financial literacy or entrepreneurship training into their day-to-day instructional plans. The very communities that need the training the most are the least likely to receive enterprise or entrepreneurship training. Why is this?

Not only is wealth creation **not** an immediate by-product of social enterprise, but it's one of the most important metrics **not** even considered when projecting the value of a social enterprise to a community. So why the new focus on social enterprise versus traditional enterprise?

- CHAPTER FIVE QUESTIONS -

Write your responses on page 103

1. Does the community your organization serves in desire social enterprises or traditional businesses?

2. Who benefits the most from social enterprise?

3. Who brokers the relationships?

4. Who controls the capital?

5. Who owns and transfers ownership?

CHAPTER SIX

The Problem With Nonprofits
*Entrepreneurs are artists, and
the marketplace is their tapestry.*

$ $ $

"Too many good not-for-profit organizations fold
due to the lack of a good business model."
—*Charles Lee*
Good Idea. Now What? How to Move Ideas to Execution

6

The freedom to launch businesses to solve problems and create opportunity is one of the benefits that has attracted millions of people to America. The very fact that a person armed with an idea and the motivation to achieve—even without speaking English, knowing American cultural systems, or having a formal education—can develop a skill and start a business is part of the American dream. In essence, the entrepreneurial spirit and dream is connected to the American dream of freedom.

Most of the entrepreneurs I know start a business to have freedom—freedom to follow a dream, freedom from past mistakes and failures, freedom from failed relationships, and freedom from ideas that launched, sputtered and died. *Entrepreneurs want freedom to start again.* If a person wants to be free, why shackle him or her down with systems and models that are burdensome? Yet many entrepreneurs are encouraged to join or launch a nonprofit organization without a clear understanding of the typical operating system or mindset. Many nonprofit organizations become burdensome, requiring entrepreneurs to work within a system that restricts their freedom and distracts them from the original idea and dream that motivated them in the first place.

Although structure, systems and models can be helpful, if not properly implemented, they can also crush a person's influence, vision and creativity. The modern-day nonprofit leader must be alert to these often good-intentioned systems that can take an organization off course. It is often the leader of the nonprofit that runs the risk of becoming distracted by the operation versus the nonprofit's initially intended purpose. Distractions can be deadly.

During World War II, dive bombing was a common strategy used by both the Allies and Axis pilots. It required pilots to ascend to an altitude of almost 10,000 feet above their target and then literally dive down on their target and release their bombs to hit the target below. Upon descent toward their target, pilots had to have the utmost focus in order to release their bombs at the precise moment to hit their targets while being fired upon by anti-aircraft fire and enemy fighter planes. Diving toward their targets at 90-degree angles and speeds of 350-500 miles per hour in an almost vertical dive simplified the bombs' trajectory and kept the pilot focused on the target below until the bombs were released. Naval aviators had an even more arduous task of hitting enemy ships, since the ships were often moving in a zig-zag pattern at speeds of 25-30 knots, to avoid being hit by the bombs. During World War II, at the Battle of Midway in 1942, several American SBD Dauntless Dive Bomb Squadrons were completely wiped out by Japanese anti-aircraft fire and enemy fighters. However, after more than 45 dive bombers were shot down and more than 90 pilots were killed in action (KIA) or missing in action (MIA), American dive bombers finally sank or fatally damaged four Japanese aircraft carriers. Japan's loss of its aircraft carriers forever changed the course of World War II in the Pacific Theatre.

What is equally important to the sinking of the carriers is why it occurred. The very simple reason is distraction. While the American pilots were dive bombing from thousands of feet above, the Japanese fighter planes were distracted and attacked by the American torpedo bombers flying 30-50 feet above the water. This literally left the Japanese aircraft carriers completely exposed and without the fighter cover of smaller aircraft armed with machine guns and air canons, allowing the American dive bombers to accurately release their bombs on their targets. By the time the Japanese realized their mistake, all four aircraft carriers and one cruiser along with other ships, were subsequently hit and sunk, leading to the loss of almost 2,500 Japanese lives and 292 aircraft. Japan's loss of their most experienced combat pilots, aircraft carriers, and support ships devastated their position in the war, and ultimately led to America's victory in the Pacific and the Japanese surrender in 1945.

> Any tax-exempt charitable organization that does not readily provide their 990 or financial report does not deserve your financial support.

1. **Mission Distraction:**

   If nonprofit leaders are not careful, they can be distracted and lose focus on their mission. Just as the Japanese lack of *discipline* led to their *distraction* and ultimately to the *death* of many, nonprofit leaders must ensure they DO NOT lose their focus and "stay on target." Nonprofit leaders often can be distracted with their own ambition and become self-referential. This is a growing challenge with the onset of social media and the instant celebrity status many leaders crave and achieve without accomplishing anything significant.

Several years ago, while in the early stages of launching StartingUp Now, a colleague insisted that I attend a multitude of meetings in Chicago's growing business accelerator and office co-sharing communities. This was suggested to "improve my brand presence" so that others could know the accomplishments of Entrenuity. While I certainly respected my colleague's strategy, and this person only meant well, something felt completely hollow about promoting myself. Internally, I knew there was much more for me to accomplish by improving my own skills and tools. It became even more unsettling when I would see the same people, with the same self-promoting message, at different events. I grew more uncomfortable with this strategy as I was missing deadlines and opportunities to secure work that earned income.

Maybe it was my upbringing or that I was not a millennial raised with the constant access to social media, which allows a person to put everything on blast for all to see and know. Maybe it's that I came from a generation and familial culture in which a person's work was to speak for itself. If others wanted to privately or publicly acknowledge my accomplishments, by all means I was/am thankful. But to intentionally seek attention simply did not work for me. I am reminded of the Proverb, "Let someone else praise you, and not your own mouth; an outsider, and not your own lips" (New International Version, Prov. 27:2). [22] Don't become a distraction to yourself or others. Focus on the mission at hand and stay focused.

2. Financial Distraction

Financials are the foundation of a strong organization. Financial

---

22 The Bible: New International Version. International Bible Society, 1984.

transparency is fundamental—no exceptions! Without strong policies and procedures to govern financials, most organizations fail. Just as brushing your teeth is essential for your personal hygiene and the "well-being" of others, financial reporting is essential for the well-being of your organization and that of your funders or investors. Whether you are a new startup generating $15,000 in annual sales or an emerging business with $1.5 million in annual revenue, being able to provide a financial report of all activities is critical for the success of the business. Reporting structures outlined by your board and investors, along with industry guidelines, will dictate the frequency of the financial reports.

The Fundamentals of Financial Transparency

> ## Your IRS Form 990

Most nonprofits must submit their Internal Revenue Service Form 990 which reports on tax-exempt organizations, nonexempt charitable trusts, and political organizations' financial activities for the year. Think of the 990 as the "income tax" form for the organization, which must be filed annually. Just as most Americans must file their personal income taxes by April 15 each year, tax-exempt organizations must file their 990 at the end of their fiscal year. I highly recommend having the 990 prepared by a Certified Public Accountant (CPA) who has proven experience and a reputation of working with nonprofits. Depending on the type of tax-exempt structure, most tax-exempt organizations' information is public information. Let me say that again: Most 990's are public information and should be readily available for distribution or download. Any tax-exempt charitable organization that does not readily provide their 990 or financial report does not deserve your financial support. Religious-based organizations, such as churches and mosques, are not required to report their financial contributions. However, a tax-exempt ministry, parachurch organization, or religious-based nonprofits typically must submit a 990 each year. Ensuring your CPA has knowledge of the nonprofit industry is extremely important to ensure the 990 is properly filed each year. (See Reference Guide pg. 124-130 for sample 990.)

> ## Certified Bookkeeper

Identifying an experienced certified bookkeeper to handle the daily, weekly, monthly financial transactions along with the reporting is essential to the success of your business. Please note, many people often claim they have bookkeeping experience, but that claim should be evidenced by the listing of their clients and/or references or certifications they have earned. If you are in the nonprofit industry, it is NOT recommended that you provide your own bookkeeping services. Hiring an experienced, certified bookkeeper is one of the pillars of a strong organization.

Can your organization function effectively and generate its own revenue sources or will it consistently be dependent on others?

> ## Certified Public Accountant (CPA)

The CPA provides the detailed analysis of the financials. The CPA and the bookkeeper should be two separate people. While they work closely together, a good practice for accountability purposes is that they should function independently of each other. The CPA should be a licensed, experienced professional with references or a client list to testify to their level of excellence. The CPA prepares the financial reports submitted to the local, state and federal government. The CPA ensures the bookkeeper's information is accurate and correct prior to submitting. I highly recommend you find a CPA who is knowledgeable about your particular industry. The CPA must stay abreast of the change in your industry that have a direct or indirect impact on your business. Simply having someone who is a CPA is not good enough. Finding someone who has experience and expertise in your industry is one of the pillars of a strong foundation.

> ## Board of Directors

Board members are the legal governing officers for the organization. The Board of Directors is responsible for all facets of the organization and can be held legally liable for the actions of the organization and its officers. The Board of Directors should not be involved in the daily operations of the organization. The Board of Directors usually is responsible for the hiring of the Chief Executive Officer (CEO) in a for-profit company or the Executive Director (ED) in a tax-exempt organization. Identifying persons with proven character, professional experience, and/or knowledge of your organization's industry to serve as board members helps the CEO/ED operate an effective organization. Many boards often have persons with experience in accounting, legal, technology, and other professional services that are helpful for the organization's operation.

3. Distracted by Dependency

When first launching Entrenuity, I was seeking donations for operations and programming services. Through a key relationship, I was introduced to a well-known business leader in Chicago named Charles Page. I was forewarned that Mr. Page, although several years retired, was a typical CEO—focused, decisive, and quite competent. Prior to his retirement, Mr. Page had led his publicly traded corporation through the intricate process of being acquired by a global marketplace leader. I was somewhat intimidated and nervous. He was a C Suite Executive through and through. I only had fifteen minutes of his time, and I had already used twelve minutes with introductions!

For the remaining five minutes, I walked Mr. Page through my presentation deck. He listened attentively and patiently without interruption. At the conclusion of the presentation, he simply said, "How can I be of service to your organization?" I informed him that I didn't know people of his stature and was only able to raise money by "teaching for a fee," not like others who were receiving donations to provide instruction. He listened as I explained the challenges of not being "connected" to key donors, foundations, and government grants. Upon listening to all of my excuses, he simply stated, "Don't change your model of charging for your instruction. Your ability to create revenue from both the client (school) and a donor is far more compelling for me to give to versus simply asking for money to get started." He then asked his secretary to cut a check for $15,000 toward Entrenuity—$10,000 more than I asked for!

These days 'sustainability' is a common catchphrase in nonprofit circles. Many donors, both public and private, want to know how an organization "sustains" itself. This is a fancy way of asking, "How do you generate revenue that is not dependent on my cash?" Can your organization function effectively and generate its own revenue sources or will it consistently be dependent on others? These are questions that must concern ALL nonprofit leaders. Unless a person is independently wealthy, there is an ongoing need to secure funding so the organization can function. In the coming months and years, organizations that can demonstrate greater levels of sustainability will gain greater levels of financial support. Organizations locked into dying models of fundraising will do exactly that. They will die out and be remembered not for their great accomplishments but for not making the necessary pivots to stay competitive in an industry that is moving toward innovation segmentation.

Financial sustainability that is dependent on taxpayer dollars is in an even more precarious tension. At the time of this writing, I have never successfully received a federal, state, or municipal grant. When I first launched Entrenuity I can certainly recall chasing the dollars, submitting multiple proposals, and never being successful at securing taxpayer funding.

If you are receiving taxpayer dollars via municipal, state, or federal grants, be prepared to face more scrutiny regarding how you organization would survive without taxpayer dollars. There is a growing trend among private foundations and individual philanthropists to limit their donations or not to donate at all if the organization cannot generate a certain level of revenue.

The American dive bombers at Midway had to "stay on target" to accomplish their mission of destroying Japanese aircraft carriers. They had to maintain total focus on their targets while diving at speeds of more than 350 miles per hour in the face of enemy anti-aircraft fire and fighter planes intent on shooting them down. In the same way, nonprofit leaders must "stay on target" to accomplish their mission, in spite of distractions. Distractions can kill. Distractions cost the lives of thousands of Japanese aviators and sailors. Distractions can lead to a nonprofit losing complete focus on its organizational mission. In light of the scenarios above, whether you are a church, nonprofit, ministry, or mosque, it is within your organizational interest to not let financial resources distract or redirect you from your mission. Sustainable programmatic activity can help keep your organization financially afloat. Your organization must keep the 3 D's in mind: Distractions can lead to Distrust, which may lead to Dysfunction.

- CHAPTER SIX QUESTIONS -

Write your responses on page 105

1. What is currently distracting your organization?

2. Who is your leadership accountable to, and what systems are in place to ensure the leader complies?

3. Does money dictate your mission?

4. What financial disciplines can you commit to and measure?

5. How does your organization "stay on target" and not lose sight of its missional focus?

   - How is this monitored, measured, and maintained?
   - What parameters are set up to avoid distractions?

6. Create a graph for the following amounts of revenue from your income statement and determine what percent of your revenue comes from:

   - Private donations or gifts
   - Sustainable revenue
   - Government (local, state, or federal)

7. What percent of resources, financial and human, is expended on the monster "fundraising" versus the ministry "programs and direct service"?

8. Which of your programmatic activities generate revenue for the organization?

9. Which programmatic activities are not sustainable and may need to be cut?

10. Based on your own findings and assessment, does this funding model lead to long-term sustainability or further dependence?

CHAPTER SEVEN

Another Way - The 70/30 Principle

$ $ $
"We pretend that success is exclusively a matter of individual merit. But there's nothing in any of the histories we've looked at so far to suggest things are that simple."
—*Malcolm Gladwell*
Outliers The Story of Success

7

Years ago, I was invited to apply for a grant. As part of the review process, my financials were analyzed, in particular, my revenue versus expenses. The committee reviewed our increase in the level of services and the number of youth and adults trained, but they were fixated on the fact that my expenses did not significantly increase. In fact, when our revenue increased, our expenses actually decreased, and they wanted to know how and why. Over the course of several years, I was able to create Program Related Income (PRI) for the programs we operated. It was simple; my goal was to only allow my expenses to consume 30% of my annual organizational budget.

Earning the 70%

Earning revenue via private donations; federal, state, or municipal grants; or PRI income are all methods of generating revenue to operate. However, there is only a limited amount of revenue available that many nonprofits compete for. Yeah, I said it—"compete" for. If you fail to understand that you are in competition with other organizations doing similar programmatic activities, you are failing to understand how the nonprofit industry works. When a foundation announces a Request for Proposal (RFP), it is an open competition for their financial dollars and in some instances to develop a relationship with the foundation and it officers. As part of the evaluation process, how your organization generates revenue and spends money is scrutinized.

Organizations that can generate 70% of their own revenue have a survival rate of more than 60% for the first 5 years of their operational life. Characteristics of organizations that meet the 70% threshold are as follows:

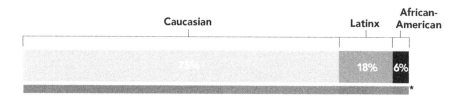

1. Leadership has a Bachelor of Arts degree or higher
2. Leadership has work experience outside of the nonprofit industry
3. Leadership relies on private family wealth
4. Most founders are younger than 40 years old

*Founders are 63% female and 37% male

Below are basic steps to audit how your organization generates revenue:

1. Secure a copy of your previous years' operational budget for the past 1-3 years from your executive director or finance department. This information is usually listed in the annual report, too.

2. Secure your organization's IRS Form 990 (see Reference Guide pg. 124-130) by looking up the nonprofit by name on Candid.org or other sites that list 990's.

3. Once you have the 990, you can find how much income the organization reported for a fiscal year.

4. Now that you have that number, identify the income sources for the revenue. On your 990, go to Part VIII, Statement of Revenue, that lists out the sources of income (i.e., foundations, private donors, grants—federal, state, municipal) or Program Related Income (PRI).

5. Using our sample 990, you can see that ACME received $100,000 from the following sources:

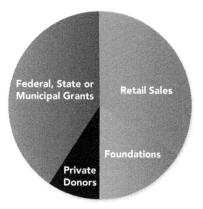

a. 30% income from rental space

b. 20% income from foundations

c. 40% income from federal, state, or municipal grants

d. 10% income from private donors

6. Now that you have determined the sources of the income, you may actually be able to determine the source by name. Go to the 990 section, and you should see a listing of the investors by name and the amount they gave.

Knowing what the investor values, their giving commitment and the frequency of their gift helps you to create a profile of them as an investor. Believe me, they may already have a profile of you if they've invited you to apply!

Work It Out

Now that you've determined ACME's revenue received, follow the steps to determine your organization's income sources and answer the following questions.

1. What are the sources for your organization's income?

2. What percent of income comes from your PRI?

3. Did you meet the 70% principle of income generation for sustainability?

4. If you did not pass the principle, what steps are necessary for your organization to pass the sustainability test?

5. Is each team member aware of his or her value and cost to the organization?

6. How is that communicated to each team member?

7. How are team members involved with creating budgets for his or her own department?

8. Is each team member aware of how his or her employment impacts the bottom-line?

9. How does that information impact the planning of budgets and performance reviews?

The 30%

Many nonprofits face the ongoing challenge of raising operational funds i order to operate their organization. These operational funds are fixed expenses such as salaries and benefits, payroll expenses, rent, utilities, and other monthly fixed costs required to operate. Operational expenses, while necessary, must be managed with keen oversight. This is an ongoing challenge for the leadership to keep expenses down and revenue up.

Spend Less/Earn More or Track Employee Expenses – Trust & Transparency

Investors do not like to see out-of-control spending or poor fiscal management. Controlling expenses is a necessary requirement to create revenue efficiencies and is more of a discipline than an art. Managing expenses requires the following:

1. Tracking the cost of labor: Paying people is often the most expensive cost in either a nonprofit or for-profit business. Tracking the cost of labor for one hour of service for an employee helps to manage one of your most expensive fixed costs—labor. If a person works for you, you should be able to track his or her cost to the organization based on either his or her hourly rate or annual salary. Knowing his or her fixed cost helps to assign a trackable value to the organization. I always recommend that any employee know his or her value and how his or her value contributes to the bottom line or, another way to put it, how to "cover their own cost." To cover your cost, you must know your cost to the organization by following one of the models below to determine the following:

   - If you are a salaried employee, divide your annual salary by two, and that will give you your approximate hourly rate. *For example, if a salaried employee earns $40,000 annually, they can follow the above example and find out they earn approximately $20.00 per hour notwithstanding payroll expenses and benefits.*

   - If you are an hourly employee, the reverse helps determine your approximate annual salary. *For example, if you are an hourly employee earning $15.00 per hour, multiply your hourly rate by two, and you can gauge that your annual salary would be approximately $30,000.*

2. Departmental Expense Tracking/Project Tracking: Many organizations do not track the cost of an employee's hours for projects within his or her own department or if the employee is working on a project in another department. For example, Rickey's Coffee Shop has an upcoming concert, and their event team is responsible for the concert. The event team is short on staff and needs Courtney, a non-barista who works as an administrative assistant, to help canvas the neighborhood and drop off posters and pluggers to advertise the concert. The event team is effectively "buying" Courtney's time from the administration department at Courtney's hourly rate of $17.00 per hour. If Courtney provides ten hours of service, the administration department has earned $170.00 in labor. The event team must account for Courtney's labor cost when planning their budget since the administration team will charge the event team. Conversely, if the administration department fails to account for Courtney's time, they will lose money from the loss of her time not spent on her administrative responsibilities.

Time Audits

There are several apps and project-tracking software resources that allow a person to budget, monitor, and track expenses to determine if a project is profitable or if it is losing money. If you do not have access to the software, See Reference Guide on pg. 123 for a simple chart that allows a person to track his or her time in 30-minute intervals. By tracking project time, you are able to identify not only the value of the project but areas of both efficiencies and inefficiencies. I recommend organizations conduct a time audit annually to determine how staff time is being used administratively by project and by program (see Reference Guide, pg. 131).

CHAPTER EIGHT

Problems Present Entrepreneurial Opportunity

Marketplace Leaders Don't Create Excuses; They Create Solutions

$ $ $

"Change will not come if we wait for some other person or some other time. We are the ones we've been waiting for. We are the change that we seek."

—*Barack Obama, President of the United States*

8

In 2005, Hurricane Katrina forced many people in New Orleans to become entrepreneurs. Katrina was the costliest natural disaster and one of the five deadliest hurricanes in the history of the United States. More than 1,200 people died in the hurricane and subsequent floods, making it the deadliest United States hurricane since the 1928 Okeechobee Hurricane. Total property damage was estimated at $108 billion (2005 USD), roughly four times the damage wrought by Hurricane Andrew in 1992 in the United States.[23] As buildings were covered in 10 feet of water, business activity stopped. The entire infrastructure of New Orleans, including commerce centers, personal dwellings, and entire industries, was completely shattered. Yet the entrepreneurial culture of New Orleans is now one of the most vibrant in the United States.

In 2007, two years after Hurricane Katrina, I was riding high! I had successfully operated our 3rd Annual Entrenuity Summer Business Camp at Wheaton College with more than 50 African-American and Latinx students learning the fundamentals of business planning and teamwork. We exceeded our fundraising goal for the camp, and everything was AWESOME! Several staff members remarked that the camp had a "spiritual-like experience" due to the uniqueness of each student and the gelling of our team. PBS filmed a documentary entitled *These Kids Mean Business*, which featured our camp and students Stephan Hall and Delano Taylor, who launched a snack business and earned $30,000 before graduating from 8th grade. It was our best year programmatically and financially to date!

Around this same time, the iPhone was being introduced, and I was learning about Facebook. I quickly realized there was a growing potential for entrepreneurship

23 Blake, Erick S, et al. "THE DEADLIEST, COSTLIEST, AND MOST INTENSE UNITED STATES TROPICAL CYCLONES FROM 1851 TO 2010 (AND OTHER FREQUENTLY REQUESTED HURRICANE FACTS)." Most Extreme Tropical Cyclones, National Hurricane Center, 2011, www.nhc.noaa.gov/dcmi.shtml

education and connecting to students well beyond programs and camps. Just as Hurricane Katrina forced New Orleans' residents and businesses to adopt new business models, the iPhone, Facebook and other social media platforms forced businesses to adapt to the new culture of instant access and constant alerts and updates at all times. The new norm of social media, like many disruptors, can enhance or inhibit productivity depending on how it is embraced.

The Pick Up

Later that year, I was picking up the second installment of a large donation from a new donor. As I walked into his office, I was feeling on edge from listening to rumors of a possible financial recession on talk radio broadcasts. (A few hours later, the news updates were even less encouraging; this was real.) This particular donor was a no-nonsense kind of a guy. After providing him with both the programmatic and financial update for our first fiscal quarter, he very seriously exhorted me, "Our country is getting ready to go through a financial crisis, something we've not experienced or seen since the financial collapse of the 1920s. I know you've just had your most successful quarter, but you must prepare for what's coming." By this time, I knew something had seriously gone wrong. He took my income statement and drew a line through the revenue and said, "Take your total revenue and cut it by 50% for the coming year. Now take that number and reduce it by another 50% for the following year (2008). If you're still around by year three (2009), cut that revenue number by 50% as well. By then the market may have bottomed out." I had nothing to say; I just looked at him and knew change was coming.

Texting & StartingUp Now

Receiving this warning about what is now known as the historic housing crash of 2008 kept me up most of the night. I tried to believe in the mantras I regularly told the youth, such as, "Believe it and achieve it," or one of my favorites to this day, "Pain is just weakness coming out of your body." I reread biblical passages trying to assure myself that everything would be all right, but nothing worked. I couldn't focus. I didn't believe, and I needed to figure out my next steps. That night, I read 1 Samuel 16. I recalled one fact in particular from the story of David and Goliath that can easily be forgotten. Even though God had selected David to be King of Israel, anointed him in front of his family, and gave him victory over Goliath, it would take David fourteen long, bloody, and brutal years before he ascended to the throne.

This is the backdrop of my mental makeup that night. Why would God allow me to have such a successful year impacting the youth and their families only to be forewarned about pending hardship?

Later in the week, I was invited to lead a workshop on entrepreneurship for students at a Chicago public school. This was nothing new, as I had led workshops and spoken to large numbers of high school students for a year. But in light of what I was going through, I felt inadequate to do the "rah rah" session on the benefits of entrepreneurship that I would normally do. Students have an uncanny ability to determine if an adult, particularly an adult on stage, is "real" or "phony," and they will let you know! Therefore, I was wide awake once again thinking of what I would say. What occurred next is totally out of custom for me being up in the middle of the night—almost in a dream state, I took out a sheet of paper and began writing down abbreviations of the keywords for sections common in a business plan. I literally just started writing "EXE" for Executive Summary, "MKTG" for Marketing, "MIS" for Mission Statement, "VIS" for Vision, and so on. I'm not sure how much time elapsed while I completed those abbreviations, but they changed everything. In the morning, I rewrote each abbreviation on one side of a 3 x 5 index card with a short 1-2 sentence definition on the back of each card.

I arrived at the school, made my way through security, and met with the principal who escorted me to the auditorium. The students began loudly arriving. After I was introduced, I began my normal presentation about entrepreneurship that involved brainteasers and monetary prizes, which definitely got their attention. When I switched subjects and began *lecturing* about business planning as life planning, the students immediately lost interest and began rudely speaking to each other as if I was no longer on stage. I took out the sheet of paper and the 3 x 5 cards with the abbreviations/definitions. I held the EXE card up over my head to get their attention and asked, "What does EXE mean?" They slowly began to refocus on me. "Whoever can answer what EXE stands for will get a soft buck ($10.00)!" I now had all of their attention back on me. Nobody answered. I then told them EXE stands for Executive Summary and gave a short definition of an executive summary. I held up another card and asked, "What does MIS mean?" Again, no one answered. "MIS stands for Mission Statement," and I gave the definition. Their frustration of not knowing and not being able to get the $10.00 got their utmost attention. I then proceeded the exercise with the remaining cards I had on hand. To this day, I do not know how many cards I had with me

I then gave them the ultimate challenge: "Whoever can tell me the abbreviation and definition of each card in order will get $20.00!" What happened next even blew the principal away. Students began working with each other. The fervor in the room grew, and student by student stood up and gave their best attempt to recite the abbreviations and definitions in order. Then a student said, "Man, this is some bull----! This is just like TEXTING on my phone! It's a code!" I promptly asked him to give an explanation. He said that the abbreviations for the business plan sections were just like abbreviations for words when people text. Several students loudly agreed with him, a few took out their flip phones, and others wrote on paper and began writing/typing the abbreviations AND the definitions! One student with phone in hand stood up and recited each of the abbreviations and definitions in order. The audience was TURNT UP to say the least, celebrating her success as she promptly marched up on stage and received her $20.00 while beaming with pride! The students wanted me to repeat the exercise, but I was out of cash! The entire presentation lasted for about 45 minutes, and the students soon left the auditorium, returning to their classrooms with their teachers. It was a great time!

Over the next year, I wrote out the abbreviations, definitions, follow-up questions, and words of wisdom more completely. What started as scribbled abbreviations on a sheet of paper evolved into a manuscript and then finally my first book, *StartingUp Now: 24 Steps to Launch Your Own Business* (SUN: 24)[24], self-published in 2011. SUN: 24 became the cornerstone for the entire StartingUp Now entrepreneurship learning system that includes the *StartingUp Now Facilitator Guide*[25] and the StartingUp Now Work Cards. In 2013, we would leverage the emergence of online communities and learning platforms and launch the first version of the StartingUp Now Skillcenter, which contained the entire *SUN: 24* workbook along with a template for users to write, research, and connect with other entrepreneurs in the United States and abroad. Prior to publishing the final version of *SUN: 24*, we hired a focus group to get input on the pros/cons of *SUN: 24*. The focus group's input was extremely valuable, leading to *SUN: 24* being condensed to 99-pages, small enough to fit in a narrow briefcase or purse,

24 Jenkins, L. Brian. Starting up Now: 24 Steps to Launch Your Own Business. StartingUp Business Solutions, 2011.
25 Jenkins, L. Brian. Starting up Now Facilitator Guide. StartingUp Business Solutions, 2011.

and easy enough for both youth and adults to understand, even without formal business training. During the focus group, a person remarked, "This isn't just for kids but for me." This was not necessarily a surprise since many parents of students I taught, especially in the community-based after school programs, would often sit in class with their students, learning side by side.

Over the last twelve years since the warning of the crash of the economy and what I perceived to be impending doom for Entrenuity, StartingUp Now's (SUN) emergence has produced revenues that have helped provide financial support for Entrenuity. SUN is set up as a separate for-profit company and as of 2018 has sold more than 10,000 units of *SUN: 24* books and related products/services. With the third iteration of the StartingUp Now Skillcenter (SC3), the SUN platform serves as a learning platform for youth and adults, new and seasoned entrepreneurs and high schools, along with being used as an accredited curriculum at several colleges, universities, corporations, prisons, and with individual users worldwide.

Problems have been proven to stir a spirit of creation. The economic crisis forced me into a creative process that fueled an emerging sustainability model of nonprofits owning for-profit businesses. The revenue model of nonprofits owning a product/service that the marketplace will pay for lessens the nonprofit's dependence on donors or taxpayers' dollars. A few years ago, I adopted a well-known acronym while preparing to speak at a conference. I wanted to come up with a highly charged acronym that would WOW the crowd and deem me a so-called "thought leader" that others would tweet about. Instead, my most innovative brainstorming session only came up with PSA, which most of us know as "Public Service Announcement." However, I edited it for my purpose to stand for "Problem, Solution, Action." This is the framework that I've adapted to view both challenges and opportunities. I believe EVERY challenge provides an entrepreneurial opportunity—you just have to TRAIN your vision to SEE the opportunity and execute!

PROBLEM: DEFINE THE PROBLEM – What is the problem that you are addressing? *In under one minute, verbally articulate the problem using the questions below:*
1. Who is being impacted by the problem?

2. Do those impacted by the problem view it as a problem or is this simply your perspective?

3. What is your motivation in addressing the problem?

4. What's in it for you?

5. Can this problem be turned into an opportunity and who benefits most?

SOLUTION: *In under one minute, state your solution using the questions below:*

1. What actions can you take to address the problem?

2. Do you have the skills, resources, and requisite training to provide a solution?

3. Can the solution scale and create further opportunity?

4. What metrics will be used to measure the success or failure of the solution?

5. Can you give your solution away so that others can benefit?

ACTION: *In under two minutes, state your market place actions using the questions below:*

1. What are the execution steps?

2. How much time do you have to execute?

3. Who is on the team, and what is their relative experience?

4. Can the plan scale and replicate?

5. Why launch this as a nonprofit versus a for-profit?

CHAPTER NINE

Character Based Leadership
*Our lives begin to end the day we
become silent about things that matter.*

$ $ $

"As a man thinketh in his heart, so is he"
—Proverbs 23.7

9

There is a leadership crisis in our country. The desire for principled leaders, filled with integrity and overflowing with truth, is needed at this present time. Such leaders, not without their sins and flaws, are humble enough to admit their failures, yet principled enough to seek forgiveness when mistakes are made. *There is no leader that is immune to character failures.* In fact, if you are a leader, a principled leader, expect your character to be challenged early and often. Whether you are serving in an obscure location or if you have a public platform, your ethic will be challenged both overtly and covertly. The challenge is not *if* your character will be challenged but *when*. The greater question is: how will you respond? Know your personal weaknesses, temptations, and ambitions. Those dark secrets that you don't disclose, not even to your spouse, are the areas most vulnerable to exploitation.

The United States military has a school that many pilots and elite soldiers participate in called Survival, Evasion, Resistance, and Escape (SERE).[26] The real SERE, not the Siri on Apple devices! The school is designed to teach military members, military contractors, and Department of Defense civilian survival skills, training in evading capture, and the military's Code of Conduct. The mental and physical anguish experienced by all SERE students is so severe that SERE's tactics were investigated by a Congressional Committee. Over a period of several days, trainees experience sleep deprivation, hunger, and abandonment, and those captured are subjected to enhanced interrogation techniques. The training is designed to push each trainee to their threshold of breaking and quitting on themselves, their team, and their country. *The discovery? Every person HAS a breaking point.* SERE training pushes the trainee to the proverbial "Edge of the Abyss" but helps trainees figure out how to no

---

26 Olsen, Erik. "SERE Training Develops Leaders for Complex Environment." Www.army.mil, 21 Nov. 2014, www.army.mil/article/138765/SERE_training_develops_leaders_for_complex_environment/

go over the edge. SERE's techniques historically derive from military personnel who were captured, tortured, and survived at the hands of their enemies in various wars and conflicts since World War II. SERE's tactics are extreme, intentionally taxing, and without compromise.

In my experience, most leadership books focus on the steps for success, not the consequences of leadership failure. That doesn't sell. However, history is replete with leaders whose failures have destroyed nations. Their ambitions, personal pride, and self-interests have created consequences others had to endure years after their death or departure. I am not aware of a SERE-type training for nonprofit leaders. The lack of such a training, particularly for nonprofit leaders, has led to many leaders compromising their standards and compromising their values, often resulting in failing their organizations, failing their families, and failing themselves.

I'm often asked: What are the core elements of success? My answer is very simple—it begins and ends with a person's character. A person's character is known through what they value. Integrity is a by-product of a person's character (which screams in silence about what they most value). Integrity can come from the core of one's character. Your values, guided by your character, direct all of your actions regardless of the circumstance. *You typically follow wherever your character leads you.*

I had a great childhood, filled with adventure and youthful mischievousness. I enjoy telling stories of my "adventures" to my children and others who are often in disbelief at how much fun I had being a kid growing up in the late 1970s and early 1980s in Berry Court sub-division in Waukegan, IL. However, it must be stated that I grew up with a father who demanded accountability, reinforced with hands-on discipline. Consequences were often talked through, ensuring I fully understood why I was being punished, followed by painful "hands-on" disciplinary actions, along with a punishment for 2-4 weeks or a restriction of my freedom, which sometimes hurt more than the hands-on discipline itself. There was always a consequence for actions both good and bad. Throughout my childhood and adolescence, my dad would always say, "Baseball players run with baseball players, football players run with football players, and fools run with fools. You must make a choice about the company you keep and who influences you." This truth was ingrained within me and has never left me. I learned excuses were unacceptable. I learned I was responsible for my actions and that those who I hung out with would have an impact on the choices I made. I learned I was accountable for my decisions.

Recently I learned of an organizational leader whose character has been compromised. Multiple levels of trust had been violated. When confronted with the truth, he did not seek to right the wrong; he was more concerned about a short-term fix versus solving the root problem. Others pointed out solutions, and he gave the appearance of wanting to do right, often saying what someone needed to hear, all the while intentionally misinforming and misrepresenting the truth. Honesty and integrity were just verbal caresses. This person's struggle with telling the truth was an admittedly learned behavior bolstered by a portion of his career spent in politics. By his own admission, he struggled with "telling the whole truth." While knowing what was right, he chose to take a short-term solution that impacted his life and many others professionally and personally. The compromises began much like a stone cutter creating a sculpture with a hammer and chisel—one chip at a time. Once the stone cutter finishes the sculpture, the finished piece usually bears no resemblance to the original block of stone. Similar to Anakin Skywalker's transformation into the dreaded Darth Vader of the *Star Wars* films' lore, Anakin's transfiguration was so complete that he physically barely resembled Anakin Skywalker. Vader's complete disfigurement was indicative of his complete depravity. The allure of power and position has entrapped many leaders who often do not realize they are being disfigured until the transformation is complete.

We must be overly conscious of those persons and systems that influence our character. On initial review, it may not seem that our values are being displaced. However, upon closer inspection, especially by those experienced in knowing what to look for, one can usually identify the tragedy before the fall.

- CHAPTER NINE QUESTIONS -

Write your responses on page 108

1. What is your definition of good character?

2. What is the source of your definition of good character?

3. How will you guard your character?

4. What are the causes of corrupted character that you've witnessed or heard about?

5. Who are you accountable to?

CHAPTER TEN

Learning to Listen, Learning to Lead

$ $ $

"Leadership and learning are indispensable to each other."
—*John F. Kennedy*
President of the United States

10

L. Brian Jenkins, U.S. Army

In the summer of 1988, while a student at the University of Iowa (Go Hawks!), I joined the United States Army Reserve Officer Training Corp, commonly known as ROTC. I selected 11 Bravo, the Infantry, as my Military Occupational Specialty (MOS). As part of my commitment, I spent weeks in Basic Training and Advanced Infantry Training (AIT) at Fort Benning, Georgia, the Home of the Infantry. While sitting with my dad on our front porch steps in the early dawn, waiting for the recruiter to pick me up for my flight to Fort Benning, my dad shared some advice that would save my life. "While in Vietnam, I saw more people killed and wounded simply for not following directions." He was stoically serious, with no expression or emotion in his voice. "Whatever the drill sergeant tells you to do, do it. Don't question, don't think, don't hesitate. React and just do what you're told. Doing what you're told will save your life and those around you."

My dad served as a Forward Observer/Radio Operator for the 155 Self-Propelled Guns out of 29 Palms California, attached to the 2nd Battalion, 3rd Division (Mar. Div.) of the United States Marine Corps. The 155 Guns supported Gulf, Hotel, Foxtrot and India Companies, as well as Force Recon, as needed on 24/7 basis. My dad volunteered—he wasn't drafted—at the age of 19 and served two tours in Vietnam from 1966-1968, fighting in the major battles of Khe Sanh, Hue City, Phu Bai, Hill 881 North and several others. Serving his country, particularly in the Marines, was one of his greatest sacrifices that he never spoke of until much later in his life. In fact, that conversation in the early morning hours before I left for Basic Training was one of the rare occurrences where he ever talked about Vietnam. My dad had my complete attention that morning more than 30 years ago, and I went on to follow his instruction. I listened and did what I was told. My life and the lives of others around me and under my leadership were dependent on the decisions and actions I made. Not listening and not obeying were not options.

The challenge many leaders face today, particularly in the nonprofit culture, is that they typically do not listen. Those who do, listen to leaders who have accomplished nothing, leaders with little to no experience or credibility to give advice to others. They listen to leaders who have had no scars, leaders who have had "no test" in their "testimony."

Lawrence S. Jenkins, U.S. Marine Corps

They have never risked anything or broken a fingernail in the service of their country or community. They are often self-referential, narcissistic, and focused solely on their social media profile, the number of likes they have on Twitter, or their number of followers.

Leadership demands more than a popular social media profile. Leadership demands substance, credibility, and oftentimes sacrifice. I am reminded of Jesus admonishing Peter, who was overly anxious to lead for many of the same reasons that many of us seek the leadership mantle. Through Jesus' hands-on instructions and actions, Peter learned that leadership has a price. Almost 30 years later, long after the execution of Jesus, tradition states that Peter was crucified by the Romans upside down per his own request because he felt unworthy to be crucified like Jesus.

Leadership is not for the weak. In fact, leadership challenges will reveal your true character. What is your motivating factor for launching your business or ministry? Is it only to gain profitability? Is there a greater good that you are seeking to solve or is the good only your bottom line? Building businesses and organizations that are "built to last" requires leaders who are "built to last." Jim Collins, in his book, *Good to Great*, found that companies that survived cultural transitions, takeovers, and restructuring all had one thing in common—leaders who listened and were adaptable.[27]

---

27 Jim Collins, Good to Great and the Social Sectors: Why Business Thinking Is Not the Answer (Jim Collins, 2005), 41-64.

- CHAPTER TEN QUESTIONS -

Write your responses on page 110

1. How are you a leader who listens?

2. How is your leadership style adaptable?

4. What areas in your leadership need improvement?

5. Who are you accountable to?

CHAPTER ELEVEN

Know More Nonprofits

$ $ $

"If you're always trying to be normal,
you'll never know how amazing you can be."
—*Maya Angelou*

11

I have been in the nonprofit industry for many years. Over these years and in this space, I've met phenomenal people who are committed to a mission of service that has allowed me to be both humbled and hopeful. I've learned many things, made some mistakes, and by the grace of God, avoided others. I've discovered that:

1. There are countless organizations seeking to do good with a limited understanding of "why their organizations are set up as nonprofits in the first place."

2. Those in the nonprofit industry must be dedicated to a disciplined approach in order to survive. Knowing the industry giants and influencers is paramount to sustainability, success, and scalability.

3. Understanding our history as a nation impacts our approach to fundraising and doing good.

4. America has an obligation to invest in its Black citizens in the key areas of:

   - Black Humanity
   - Black Male Personhood
   - Black Womanhood
   - Black Economic Opportunity
   - Black Legislation
   - Black Educational Opportunities

5. Indigenous leaders of churches and ministries should be trained and ultimately positioned to have a direct relationship with CEOs, sponsors, and private funders, rather than a filtered third- or fourth-tiered relationship simply as a recipient of generosity.

6. The ability to create wealth or pass down wealth is the common denominator to communities becoming economically stable. Th

very principles that help majority Caucasian/white-led ministries raise money can impede wealth creation for Black and brown people.

7. Many nonprofit organizations become burdensome, requiring entrepreneurs to work within a system that restricts their freedom and distracts them from the original idea and dream that motivated them in the first place. The modern-day nonprofit leader must be alert to these often good-intentioned systems that can take an organization off course.

8. Organizations that can generate 70% of their own revenue have a survival rate of more than 60% for the first five years of their operational life.

9. EVERY challenge provides an entrepreneurial opportunity—you just have to TRAIN your vision to SEE the opportunity and execute a plan of action to solve the problem!

10. No leader is immune to character failures. The challenge is not if your character will be challenged but when. The greater question is: how will you respond?

11. Leadership challenges will reveal your true character. Building businesses and organizations that are "built to last" requires leaders who are "built to last."

Most of the people I've had the privilege to know in the nonprofit industry have a vision to serve that, regardless of financial support, has never been based on the bottom line. It's simply about serving and doing good. Many of these people are leaders in their chosen area of influence. Some are returning citizens, and some are CEOs. Regardless of their status in life, their common bond is service. I'm hopeful that the challenges and opportunities many of us have overcome will be an encouragement for new leaders. I hope that we will open opportunities, craft and curate relationships and inspire others. I hope that future leaders will be conscious of our nation's history but not let that history be a barrier to progress. Although our country has a horrendous history in its treatment of Black people, I'm hopeful that the pride and resiliency of Black people will be a perpetual encouragement for future generations and leaders of all ethnicities. Black progress is American progress, and American progress is Black progress. Doing good can be done in a way that is respectful, that deliberately invests in people and communities, and that creates wealth, sustainability, and independence if we just KNOW more.

AFTERWORD

In 2019 we will celebrate Entrenuity's 20th Anniversary, which is a huge milestone. I was not even aware of the pending anniversary until I started planning for 2019, which is a very important year for me both professionally and personally. Our eldest daughter, Bria, is getting married, my wife and I will celebrate our 25th anniversary, and Entrenuity turns 20! I've never been big on celebrating professional milestones up to this point for a very simple reason—I was still laying the foundation to actually have something to celebrate! Pseudo celebrations where nothing has been accomplished do not work for me. Celebrating often causes reflection. Our memories are triggered by significant events. Whether these events are helpful or hurtful, there is still a "mental bookmark" that allows us to easily find our significant moments. These moments have often forced us to take action. These decisions lead to actions that shape our lives personally or professionally. Entrenuity can celebrate 20 years of operations for a few key reasons that began long before Entrenuity was ever launched:

1. A strong family foundation established by Larry and Madelyn Jenkins. I grew up in a two-parent home with a father and mother who were supportive and provided a strong foundation. Their love was best demonstrated by their intentional sacrifices and "going without" so we could be positioned to do more. While their marriage sometimes struggled, their focus to provide a stable home environment never wavered. I learned sacrifice, discipline, and perseverance from them. Having been personally shaped by a strong family foundation has led to Entrenuity having a strong foundation.

2. A believing and supportive wife of almost 25 years, Jenai Jenkins, PhD. While the sacrifices and hardships experienced to launch Entrenuity were often like cataclysmic events felt by me each day, the tremors and tsunamis I brought home were equally experienced by my wife. While I was still figuring out what I was doing, my wife ALWAYS supported my work and vision. More importantly, she provided a stable home, led by a loving wife, while working a full-time job and being a great mother to our three children. A strong marriage, not without its moments of struggle, curated an environment for me and my children to be continually refreshed and renewed. It was her continual belief then and her continual belief now that has helped me position Entrenuity to create a culture of commerce. Having a supportive wife has led to Entrenuity having a strong foundation.

3. It's not about you…learning to play your position. In 1989 I met Don Davis while I was going into my fourth year of undergraduate studies at the University of Iowa. Don, Beth, and their three young children were at Iowa as Don was working on his Ph.D. in Religion. Don at this time was a 10-year veteran of urban ministry, valedictorian of Wheaton College Class of 1989, and friend to many. When I met Don, I was forced to realize that my dream of serving in the United States Army Special Forces as an officer was over. I was directionless, somewhat bewildered about next steps as a student and ultimately in a profession. Up to this point, all my energy and direction had been focused on securing my commission as a second lieutenant and being assigned to a combat unit. I had sacrificed grades, relationships and values to secure that commission. When my plans were not realized, I was listless as a ship without a sail. It was at this point that I was introduced to Don. Don's ability to listen coupled with the freedom to talk out my problems helped refocus me on who I was. We shared many discussions, meals with his family, Bible studies, and just hanging out, and during one of those times he said, "Maybe all that you've experienced has nothing to do with you at all. Maybe the Lord wants to use you for His purposes, not necessarily your purposes. It's not about you, but your obedience to Him." It was that conversation and many more that followed until my graduation from the University of Iowa in 1991, that reshaped, refocused, and repurposed my life. Over the next two years, Don and I

established an Apostle Paul/Timothy relationship of the elder training the younger. It was our many engagements that helped establish the concept of Entrenuity, an organization designed for urban youth to learn the fundamentals of business planning. Entrenuity's core components were established years before I even knew the definition of what an *entrepreneur* was, much less helping people launch their dreams and ideas. Entrenuity at its core, much like my commitment to Christ, is set up to serve others. I believe it's a beautiful and interesting story that the Lord can use ANYONE to accomplish HIS purposes. Our role as servants is to be obedient and to be found faithful in the mission, purpose, and execution of HIS plans. Entrenuity was never about me; Entrenuity has always been about *you!*

The foundation of a strong family upbringing, a strong and supportive wife, strong mentors, and having a vision and belief to serve people are the driving forces for Entrenuity. Our service just happens to be in the form of entrepreneurship, which is helping create a strategy to solve problems.

As I look back on my career in entrepreneurship education, what stands out the most to me is my gratitude for those who were willing to believe in my IDEA and help me GROW … and the privilege of being able to impact the lives of others who have an IDEA and help them GROW.

QUESTIONS & NOTES

- CHAPTER ONE QUESTIONS -

1. In your community, which organizations have the most impact, nonprofits or for-profits?

_____

_____

_____

_____

_____

_____

_____

2. What has been your experience with the nonprofit industry?

_____

_____

_____

_____

_____

_____

_____

3. What has been your experience with the for-profit industry?

_____

_____

_____

_____

_____

_____

_____

4. Which industry has produced more leaders in the United States, nonprofit or for-profits?

_____

_____

_____

_____

_____

_____

5. Make a list of people who personally influence you, such as mentors, people you follow on podcasts, and other influencers. Which industry have they spent the majority of their careers in, nonprofits or for-profits?

_____

_____

_____

_____

_____

_____

_____

6. Which industry do you find more women and people of color in leadership positions, nonprofits or for-profits?

_____

_____

_____

_____

_____

_____

_____

- CHAPTER THREE QUESTIONS -

1. Has your organization experienced disinvestment or do you work in a community that has experienced generational or historical disinvestment?

_____

_____

_____

_____

_____

_____

2. How has your organization benefited from America's intentional disinvestment of Black people?

_____

_____

_____

_____

_____

_____

3. How has your organization performed intentional investment with its time, talent, influence and financial resources? What are the measurable impacts that can be reported on your organization's investment?

_____

_____

_____

_____

_____

_____

4. Of the intentional investment activities led by your organization, which are scalable and replicable?

_____

_____

_____

_____

_____

_____

_____

5. How has your organization acknowledged and/or contributed to Black Humanity?

_____

_____

_____

_____

_____

_____

6. How has your organization acknowledged and/or contributed to Black Male Personhood?

_____

_____

_____

_____

_____

_____

7. How has your organization acknowledged and/or contributed to Black Womanhood?

_____

_____

_____

_____

_____

_____

How has your organization acknowledged and/or contributed to Black Economic Opportunity?

_____
_____
_____
_____
_____
_____
_____

9. How has your organization acknowledged and/or contributed to Black Legislation?

_____
_____
_____
_____
_____
_____

10. How has your organization acknowledged and/or contributed to Black Educational Opportunities?

_____
_____
_____
_____
_____
_____
_____
_____
_____
_____
_____
_____

- CHAPTER FIVE QUESTIONS -

1. Does the community your organization serves in desire social enterprises or traditional businesses?

_____
_____
_____
_____
_____
_____
_____

2. Who benefits the most from social enterprise?

_____
_____
_____
_____
_____
_____

3. Who brokers the relationships?

_____
_____
_____
_____
_____
_____

. Who controls the capital?

_____
_____
_____
_____
_____
_____
_____

5. Who owns and transfers ownership?

_____

_____

_____

_____

_____

_____

_____

- CHAPTER SIX QUESTIONS -

1. What is currently distracting your organization?

_____

_____

_____

_____

_____

_____

_____

2. Who is your leadership accountable to, and what systems are in place to ensure the leader complies?

_____

_____

_____

_____

_____

_____

_____

3. Does money dictate your mission?

_____

_____

_____

_____

_____

_____

_____

4. What financial disciplines can you commit to and measure?

_____

_____

_____

_____

_____

_____

_____

5. How does your organization "stay on target" and not lose sight of its missional focus?
   - How is this monitored, measured, and maintained?
   - What parameters are set up to avoid distractions?

_____

_____

_____

_____

_____

_____

_____

6. Create a graph for the following amounts of revenue from your income statement and determine what percent of your revenue comes from:
   - Private donations or gifts
   - Sustainable revenue
   - Government (local, state, or federal)

_____

_____

_____

_____

_____

_____

_____

7. What percent of resources, financial and human, is expended on the monster "fundraising" versus the ministry "programs and direct service"?

_____

_____

_____

_____

_____

_____

8. Which of your programmatic activities generate revenue for the organization?

_____

_____
_____
_____
_____
_____
_____

9. Which programmatic activities are not sustainable and may need to be cut?

_____
_____
_____
_____
_____
_____

10. Based on your own findings and assessment, does this funding model lead to long-term sustainability or further dependence

_____
_____
_____
_____
_____
_____

- CHAPTER NINE QUESTIONS -

1. What is your definition of good character?

_____

_____

_____

_____

_____

_____

_____

2. What is the source of your definition of good character?

_____

_____

_____

_____

_____

_____

3. How will you guard your character?

_____

_____

_____

_____

_____

_____

4. What are the causes of corrupted character that you have witnessed or heard about?

_____

_____

_____

_____

_____

_____

5. Who are you accountable to?

- CHAPTER TEN QUESTIONS -

1. Are you a leader who listens?

_____
_____
_____
_____
_____
_____
_____

2. Is your leadership style adaptable?

_____
_____
_____
_____
_____
_____

3. What areas in your leadership need improvement?

_____
_____
_____
_____
_____
_____

4. Who are you accountable to?

_____
_____
_____
_____
_____
_____

- ADDITIONAL NOTES -

REFERENCE GUIDE

Top 9 Slave Holders
in U.S. History

1. Robert Francis Withers Allston: Georgia, SC. Industry: rice. Owned 690 Black slaves. 2. Col. Joshu John Ward: Georgetown County, SC. Industry: rice. Owned 1,092 Black slaves. 3. Meredith Calhour Rapides Parish, LA. Industry: cotton, sugarcane. Owned 709 Black slaves. Net worth: $1M/$31M today. 4. William Aiken: Colleton, SC. Industry: Rice, Sweet Potatoes, Corn. Owned 700 Black slave: Net Worth $3.5M /$107M today. 5. Gov. John L. Manning: Ascension, LA. Industry: cotton. Owne 670 Black slaves. 6. John Burnside: Burnside, LA. Industry: sugarcane. Owned 750 Black slaves. N worth: $5M/$154M today. 7. Stephen Duncan: Natchez, MS. Industry: Cotton, sugarcane. Owne 1,000 Black slaves. Net Worth: $3.5M/$107M today 8. Joseph and Adelicia Acklen: TN and L/ Owned 700 Black slaves. Net worth $3M/$29M today. 9. Joseph Blake (no image available): Beaufo County, SC. Industry: rice. Owned 575 Black slaves.

- BALANCE SHEET -

14. Washo Plantation To Sundry Accounts
To Benj.ᵃ Stiles, Exec.ʳ Samuel Winborn
for Negroes bo.ᵗ this Day at Pub Sale viz

Bristol	a Man	305.	
Adam	d.°	322.	
Plato	d.°	282.	
Paul	d.°	263.	
Ephraim	d.°	307.	
Tom	d.°	350.	
June	d.° Cooper	252.	
Will	d.°	334.	
Caroline	d.°	260.	
Jemmy	d.°	370.	
Sampson	d.°	238.	
Cato	d.°	400.	
Prince	d.°	303.	
Titus	a Big Boy	276.	
Sarah, & her 3 Children Jane Peggy & Cyrus	611.		
Sylvia, & her Child Dina	380.		
Chloe , d.° Charlotte	328.		
Betty , d.° Bella	333.		
Darkey , d.° Judith	365.		
Will a blind fellow	21.	6579.	

283.13.4 Rem.ᵈ

To Ed. H. Plant.ᵃ for a Blanket gave Flora
& [?] sent there for my own use . a 37/6 . . . 5. 13. 3
To John Vaux for 76 B.ᵗ Small rice, say
164 [?] a 22/6 & [?]. . . . 1. 17. 6
To Cash p.ᵈ for Provisions 10/ Negroes to carry
& 5 Negroes over the river 30/ my Exp. to South 10/ . 2. 15.

6589. 5. 9

- COMPARISON CHARTS -
Download full chart analysis at
www.startingupnow.com/KMNP_charts.pdf

Evangelical Urban Ministries in Chicago:
Race-based Revenue Comparison
Revenue listed below only includes income from urban ministries
(non-churches) based on their 2012-2013 IRS 990 filing.

TOTAL INCOME RAISED: $37,183,525

(9) White-Led Ministries (WM)
In African-American/Latinx Communities

(7) African-American/Latinx Led Ministries (ALM)
In African-American/Latinx Communities

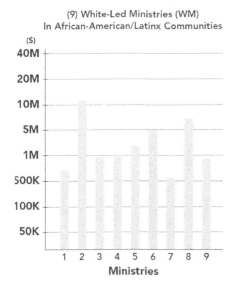

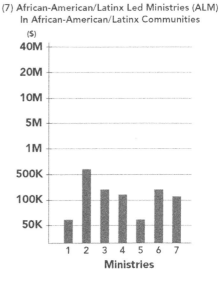

WM: $35M Total Raised

ALM: $1.7M Total Raised

REVENUE SUMMARY

WM 96%   ALM 4.01%

Evangelical Urban Ministries in Chicago:
Gender-based Revenue Comparison
White, female-led organizations raised 78% of the total income in 2012-2013, even though they represented only 25% of the organizations surveyed.

Gender Comparison: 16 Ministries
TOTAL INCOME RAISED: $37,183,525

9 White-Led Ministries (WM)
Male/Female Comparison
Funds Raised

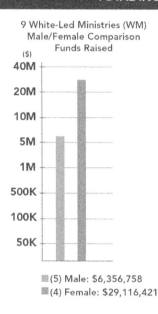

■ (5) Male: $6,356,758
■ (4) Female: $29,116,421

7 African-American and Latinx Led Ministries (ALM)
Male/Female Comparison
Funds Raised

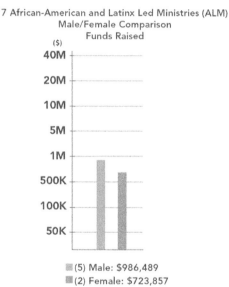

■ (5) Male: $986,489
■ (2) Female: $723,857

GENDER-BASED REVENUE SUMMARY

20%   80%

Evangelical Urban Ministries in Chicago:
Racial Comparison-Length of Operation
White-led urban ministries secured higher levels of funding overall, leading to
sustained ministry presence overall, regardless of relevance or impact in the community.

TOTAL COMPARED YEARS OF OPERATION (Founding Through 2015): 478

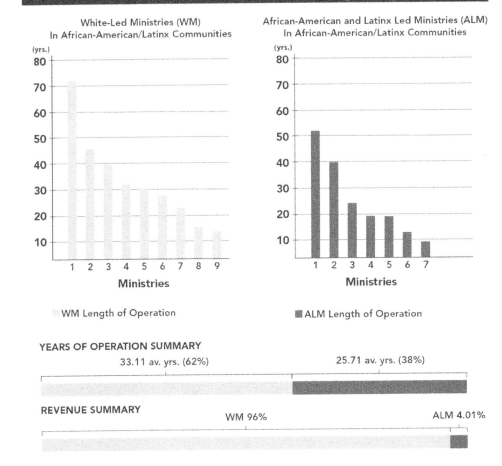

White-Led Ministries (WM)
In African-American/Latinx Communities

African-American and Latinx Led Ministries (ALM)
In African-American/Latinx Communities

Ministries

Ministries

WM Length of Operation

ALM Length of Operation

YEARS OF OPERATION SUMMARY

33.11 av. yrs. (62%)   25.71 av. yrs. (38%)

REVENUE SUMMARY

WM 96%   ALM 4.01%

Evangelical Urban Ministries in Chicago:
Racial Comparison-Length of Experience
White-led urban ministries had access to significantly higher levels of funding
in shorter time periods and in spite of less proven experience in the field.

TOTAL COMBINED YEARS OF FIELD EXPERIENCE: 51

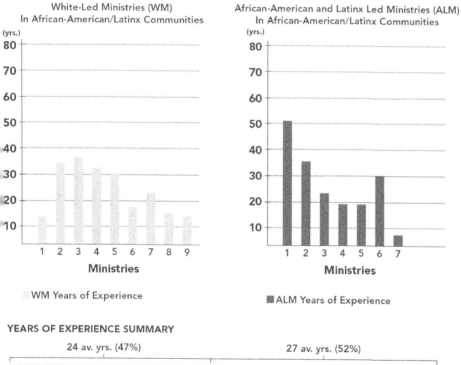

White-Led Ministries (WM)
In African-American/Latinx Communities

African-American and Latinx Led Ministries (ALM)
In African-American/Latinx Communities

Ministries

Ministries

WM Years of Experience

ALM Years of Experience

YEARS OF EXPERIENCE SUMMARY

24 av. yrs. (47%)   27 av. yrs. (52%)

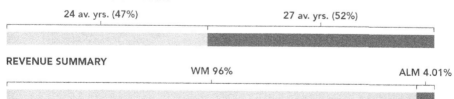

REVENUE SUMMARY

WM 96%   ALM 4.01%

Evangelical Urban Ministries in Chicago:
Racial Comparison-Education
White ministry leaders averaged more business related degrees while African-American and
Latinx ministry leaders had degrees in religious related studies, which directly impacted fundraising.

Education Comparison: 16 Ministries

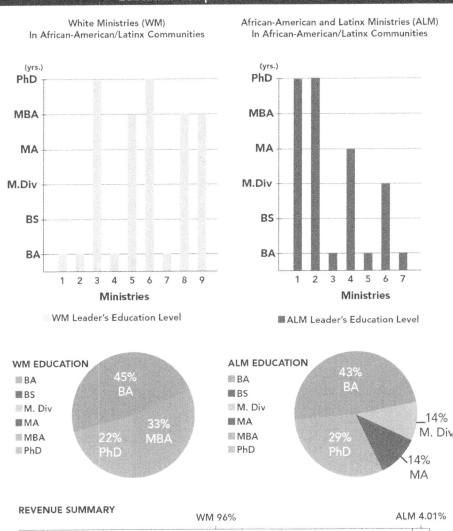

White Ministries (WM)
In African-American/Latinx Communities

African-American and Latinx Ministries (ALM)
In African-American/Latinx Communities

WM Leader's Education Level

ALM Leader's Education Level

WM EDUCATION
- BA
- BS
- M. Div
- MA
- MBA
- PhD

45% BA
33% MBA
22% PhD

ALM EDUCATION
- BA
- BS
- M. Div
- MA
- MBA
- PhD

43% BA
29% PhD
14% M. Div
14% MA

REVENUE SUMMARY
WM 96%
ALM 4.01%

Evangelical Urban Ministries in Chicago:
Racial Comparison-
Ministries Still in Operation by Original Founder*

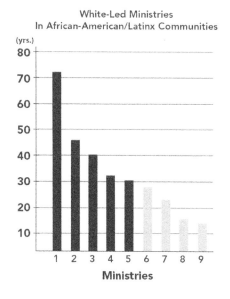

White-Led Ministries
In African-American/Latinx Communities

African-American and Latinx Led Ministries
In African-American/Latinx Communities

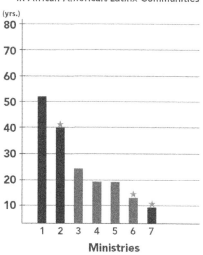

Non-Original Founder Leadership
Original Founder Leadership

Non-Original Founder Leadership
Original Founder Leadership

ORIGINAL FOUNDER LEADERSHIP SUMMARY

WM: Original Founder Leadership (44%)   ALM: Original Founder Leadership (57%)

REVENUE SUMMARY

WM 96%   ALM 4.01%

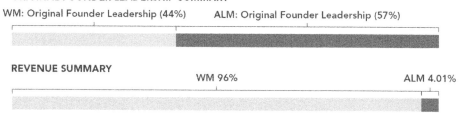

* From 1947-2015   ★ No Longer In Operation

Evangelical Urban Ministries in Chicago:
Racial Comparison-Neighborhood

White ministry leaders from outside the community raised significantly
higher levels of funding than indigenous, grassroots leaders.

Neighborhood Comparison: 16 Ministries

White Ministry Leaders (WM) Who
Grew Up In AA/Latinx Communities

	YES	NO
1		X
2		X
3		X
4		X
5		X
6		X
7		X
8		X
9		X

WM: 0%

African-American and Latinx Ministry Leaders (ALM)
Who Grew Up In AA/Latinx Communities

	YES	NO
1	X	
2	X	
3	X	
4	X	
5	X	
6	X	
7	X	

ALM: 100%

NEIGHBORHOOD ORIGINATION SUMMARY

ALM grew up in neighborhood served (100%)

REVENUE SUMMARY

WM 96%   ALM 4.01%

Evangelical Urban Ministries in Chicago:
Racial Comparison—Cultural Relevance
The cultural competence of leadership directly impacts staffing,
marketing, fundraising, community collaboration, and stability.

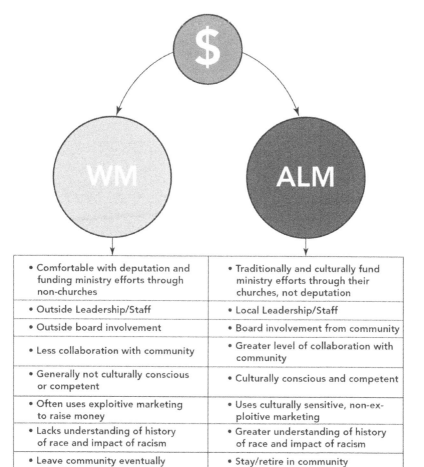

WM	ALM
• Comfortable with deputation and funding ministry efforts through non-churches	• Traditionally and culturally fund ministry efforts through their churches, not deputation
• Outside Leadership/Staff	• Local Leadership/Staff
• Outside board involvement	• Board involvement from community
• Less collaboration with community	• Greater level of collaboration with community
• Generally not culturally conscious or competent	• Culturally conscious and competent
• Often uses exploitive marketing to raise money	• Uses culturally sensitive, non-exploitive marketing
• Lacks understanding of history of race and impact of racism	• Greater understanding of history of race and impact of racism
• Leave community eventually	• Stay/retire in community

Revenue Summary

WM 96% ALM 4.01%

Know More Nonprofits

Form **8453-EO**	**Exempt Organization Declaration and Signature for Electronic Filing**	OMB No. 1545-1879
Department of the Treasury Internal Revenue Service	For calendar year 2011, or tax year beginning __ 01/01 , 2011, and ending ___ 12/31, 20 11. For use with Forms 990, 990-EZ, 990-PF, 1120-POL, and 8868 ▶ See instructions on back.	2011

Name of exempt organization	Employer identification number
EXEMPT ORGANIZATION	12-3456789

Part I Type of Return and Return Information (Whole Dollars Only)

Check the box for the type of return being filed with Form 8453-EO and enter the applicable amount, if any, from the return. If you check the box on line **1a, 2a, 3a, 4a,** or **5a** below and the amount on that line of the return being filed with this form was blank, then leave line **1b, 2b, 3b, 4b,** or **5b,** whichever is applicable, blank (do not enter -0-). If you entered -0- on the return, then enter -0- on the applicable line below. **Do not** complete more than one line in Part I

1a Form 990 check here ▶ [X]	b Total revenue, if any (Form 990, Part VIII, column (A), line 12) . . .	1b	10053000.
2a Form 990-EZ check here ▶ [ ]	b Total revenue, if any (Form 990-EZ, line 9)	2b	
3a Form 1120-POL check here ▶ [ ]	b Total tax (Form 1120-POL, line 22)	3b	
4a Form 990-PF check here ▶ [ ]	b Tax based on investment income (Form 990-PF, Part VI, line 5)	4b	
5a Form 8868 check here ▶ [ ]	b Balance due (Form 8868, Part I, line 3c or Part II, line 8c)	5b	

Part II Declaration of Officer

6 [ ] I authorize the U.S. Treasury and its designated Financial Agent to initiate an Automated Clearing House (ACH) electronic funds withdrawal (direct debit) entry to the financial institution account indicated in the tax preparation software for payment of the organization's federal taxes owed on this return, and the financial institution to debit the entry to this account. To revoke a payment, I must contact the U.S. Treasury Financial Agent at 1-888-353-4537 no later than 2 business days prior to the payment (settlement) date. I also authorize the financial institutions involved in the processing of the electronic payment of taxes to receive confidential information necessary to answer inquiries and resolve issues related to the payment.

[ ] If a copy of this return is being filed with a state agency(ies) regulating charities as part of the IRS Fed/State program, I certify that I executed the electronic disclosure consent contained within this return allowing disclosure by the IRS of this Form 990/990-EZ/990-PF (as specifically identified in Part I above) to the selected state agency(ies).

Under penalties of perjury, I declare that I am an officer of the above named organization and that I have examined a copy of the organization's 2011 electronic return and accompanying schedules and statements, and to the best of my knowledge and belief, they are true, correct, and complete. I further declare that the amount in Part I above is the amount shown on the copy of the organization's electronic return. I consent to allow my intermediate service provider, transmitter, or electronic return originator (ERO) to send the organization's return to the IRS and to receive from the IRS **(a)** an acknowledgement of receipt or reason for rejection of the transmission, **(b)** the reason for any delay in processing the return or refund, and **(c)** the date of any refund.

Sign Here ▶		04/12/2012	▶ CFO	
	Signature of officer	Date	Title	

Part III Declaration of Electronic Return Originator (ERO) and Paid Preparer (see instructions)

I declare that I have reviewed the above organization's return and that the entries on Form 8453-EO are complete and correct to the best of my knowledge. If I am only a collector, I am not responsible for reviewing the return and only declare that this form accurately reflects the data on the return. The organization officer will have signed this form before I submit the return. I will give the officer a copy of all forms and information to be filed with the IRS, and have followed all other requirements in Pub. 4163, Modernized e-File (MeF) Information for Authorized IRS *e-file* Providers for Business Returns. If I am also the Paid Preparer, under penalties of perjury I declare that I have examined the above organization's return and accompanying schedules and statements, and to the best of my knowledge and belief, they are true, correct, and complete. This Paid Preparer declaration is based on all information of which I have any knowledge.

		Date	Check if also paid preparer	Check if self-employed [X]	ERO's SSN or PTIN
ERO's Use Only	ERO's signature ▶				P00736879
	Firm's name (or yours if self-employed), address, and ZIP code ▶	EISNERAMPER LLP 750 THIRD AVENUE NEW YORK		NY 10017-2703	EIN 13-1639826 Phone no.

Under penalties of perjury, I declare that I have examined the above return and accompanying schedules and statements, and to the best of my knowledge and belief, they are true, correct, and complete. Declaration of preparer is based on all information of which the preparer has any knowledge.

	Print/Type preparer's name	Preparer's signature	Date	Check [ ] if self-employed	PTIN
Paid Preparer Use Only	Firm's name ▶			Firm's EIN ▶	
	Firm's address ▶			Phone no.	

For Privacy Act and Paperwork Reduction Act Notice, see back of form.   Form **8453-EO** (2011)

JSA
1E1675 1.000

90958W L161   4/3/2012   9:10:34 AM   V 11-4.1

Form **990**

Department of the Treasury
Internal Revenue Service

Return of Organization Exempt From Income Tax

Under section 501(c), 527, or 4947(a)(1) of the Internal Revenue Code (except black lung benefit trust or private foundation)

▶ The organization may have to use a copy of this return to satisfy state reporting requirements.

OMB No. 1545-0047

2011

Open to Public Inspection

A For the 2011 calendar year, or tax year beginning _____ , 2011, and ending _____ , 20 _____

B Check if applicable:	**C** Name of organization	**D** Employer identification number
☐ Address change	EXEMPT ORGANIZATION	12-3456789
☐ Name change	Doing Business As	
☐ Initial return	Number and street (or P.O. box if mail is not delivered to street address)	Room/suite	**E** Telephone number
☐ Terminated	1 MAIN STREET		(555) 555-5555
☐ Amended return	City or town, state or country, and ZIP + 4		
☐ Application pending	ANYCITY, NY 10001		**G** Gross receipts $ 13,603,000.

F Name and address of principal officer: EMPLOYEE A
1 MAIN STREET ANYCITY, NY 10001

H(a) Is this a group return for affiliates?	☐ Yes	☒ No
H(b) Are all affiliates included?	☐ Yes	☐ No
If "No," attach a list. (see instructions)		

I Tax-exempt status: ☒ 501(c)(3) ☐ 501(c) ( ) ◀ (insert no.) ☐ 4947(a)(1) or ☐ 527

J Website: ▶ WWW.EXEMPTORG.ORG

H(c) Group exemption number ▶

K Form of organization: ☒ Corporation ☐ Trust ☐ Association ☐ Other ▶   **L** Year of formation 1983 **M** State of legal domicile NY

Part I Summary

1 Briefly describe the organization's mission or most significant activities: ESTABLISHED TO IMPROVE THE HEALTH AND WELL-BEING OF PEOPLE LIVING WITH SERIOUS AND PERSISTENT MENTAL ILLNESSES.

2 Check this box ▶ ☐ if the organization discontinued its operations or disposed of more than 25% of its net assets.

3 Number of voting members of the governing body (Part VI, line 1a)	**3**	15.
4 Number of independent voting members of the governing body (Part VI, line 1b)	**4**	13.
5 Total number of individuals employed in calendar year 2011 (Part V, line 2a)	**5**	124.
6 Total number of volunteers (estimate if necessary)	**6**	8.
7a Total unrelated business revenue from Part VIII, column (C), line 12	**7a**	0
b Net unrelated business taxable income from Form 990-T, line 34	**7b**	0

		Prior Year	Current Year
8	Contributions and grants (Part VIII, line 1h)	9,458,000.	9,458,000.
9	Program service revenue (Part VIII, line 2g)	0	0
10	Investment income (Part VIII, column (A), lines 3, 4, and 7d)	288,000.	288,000.
11	Other revenue (Part VIII, column (A), lines 5, 6d, 8c, 9c, 10c, and 11e)	337,000.	307,000.
12	Total revenue - add lines 8 through 11 (must equal Part VIII, column (A), line 12)	10,083,000.	10,053,000.
13	Grants and similar amounts paid (Part IX, column (A), lines 1-3)	0	0
14	Benefits paid to or for members (Part IX, column (A), line 4)	0	0
15	Salaries, other compensation, employee benefits (Part IX, column (A), lines 5-10)	4,152,000.	4,062,000.
16a	Professional fundraising fees (Part IX, column (A), line 11e)	60,000.	60,000.
b	Total fundraising expenses (Part IX, column (D), line 25) ▶ 495,000.		
17	Other expenses (Part IX, column (A), lines 11a-11d, 11f-24e)	4,601,000.	4,601,000.
18	Total expenses. Add lines 13-17 (must equal Part IX, column (A), line 25)	8,813,000.	8,723,000.
19	Revenue less expenses. Subtract line 18 from line 12	1,270,000.	1,330,000.

		Beginning of Current Year	End of Year
20	Total assets (Part X, line 16)	21,301,000.	22,289,000.
21	Total liabilities (Part X, line 26)	5,857,000.	5,703,000.
22	Net assets or fund balances. Subtract line 21 from line 20	15,444,000.	16,586,000.

Part II Signature Block

Under penalties of perjury, I declare that I have examined this return, including accompanying schedules and statements, and to the best of my knowledge and belief, it is true, correct, and complete. Declaration of preparer (other than officer) is based on all information of which preparer has any knowledge.

Sign Here

▶ _____ Signature of officer   Date _____

▶ _____ Type or print name and title

Paid Preparer Use Only	Print/Type preparer's name	Preparer's signature	Date	Check ☐ if self-employed	PTIN P00736879
	Firm's name ▶ EISNERAMPER LLP			Firm's EIN ▶ 13-1639826	
	Firm's address ▶ 750 THIRD AVENUE NEW YORK, NY 10017-2703			Phone no.	

May the IRS discuss this return with the preparer shown above? (see instructions) .... ☒ Yes ☐ No

For Paperwork Reduction Act Notice, see the separate instructions.

JSA
1.000

Form **990** (2011)

90958W L161 4/3/2012 9:10:34 AM V 11-4.1

EXEMPT ORGANIZATION   12-3456789

Part III **Statement of Program Service Accomplishments**
Check if Schedule O contains a response to any question in this Part III . . . . ☐

1 Briefly describe the organization's mission:
ESTABLISHED TO IMPROVE THE HEALTH AND WELL-BEING OF PEOPLE LIVING
WITH SERIOUS AND PERSISTENT MENTAL ILLNESSES.

2 Did the organization undertake any significant program services during the year which were not listed on the
prior Form 990 or 990-EZ? . . . . ☐ Yes ☒ No
If "Yes," describe these new services on Schedule O.
3 Did the organization cease conducting, or make significant changes in how it conducts, any program
services? . . . . ☐ Yes ☒ No
If "Yes," describe these changes on Schedule O.
4 Describe the organization's program service accomplishments for each of its three largest program services, as measured by
expenses. Section 501(c)(3) and 501(c)(4) organizations and section 4947(a)(1) trusts are required to report the amount of
grants and allocations to others, the total expenses, and revenue, if any, for each program service reported.

4a (Code: _____) (Expenses $ ____3,413,000.__ including grants of $ _____) (Revenue $ _____)
PROGRAM 1 - DETAILED DESCRIPTION

4b (Code: _____) (Expenses $ ____3,000,000.__ including grants of $ _____) (Revenue $ _____)
PROGRAM 2 - DETAILED DESCRIPTION

4c (Code: _____) (Expenses $ ____1,094,000.__ including grants of $ _____) (Revenue $ _____)
PROGRAM 3 - DETAILED DESCRIPTION

4d Other program services (Describe in Schedule O.)
(Expenses $ _____ including grants of $ _____) (Revenue $ _____)
4e Total program service expenses ▶   7,507,000.

JSA
020 1 000   Form **990** (2011
90958W L161 4/3/2012   9:10:34 AM   V 11-4.1

EXEMPT ORGANIZATION   12-3456789

Form 990 (2011)   Page **3**

Part IV   **Checklist of Required Schedules**

			Yes	No
1	Is the organization described in section 501(c)(3) or 4947(a)(1) (other than a private foundation)? *If "Yes,"* *complete Schedule A*	**1**	X	
2	Is the organization required to complete *Schedule B, Schedule of Contributors* (see instructions)?	**2**	X	
3	Did the organization engage in direct or indirect political campaign activities on behalf of or in opposition to candidates for public office? *If "Yes," complete Schedule C, Part I*	**3**		X
4	**Section 501(c)(3) organizations.** Did the organization engage in lobbying activities, or have a section 501(h) election in effect during the tax year? *If "Yes," complete Schedule C, Part II*	**4**	X	
5	Is the organization a section 501(c)(4), 501(c)(5), or 501(c)(6) organization that receives membership dues, assessments, or similar amounts as defined in Revenue Procedure 98-19? *If "Yes," complete Schedule C, Part III*	**5**		
6	Did the organization maintain any donor advised funds or any similar funds or accounts for which donors have the right to provide advice on the distribution or investment of amounts in such funds or accounts? *If "Yes," complete Schedule D, Part I*	**6**		X
7	Did the organization receive or hold a conservation easement, including easements to preserve open space, the environment, historic land areas, or historic structures? *If "Yes," complete Schedule D, Part II*	**7**		X
8	Did the organization maintain collections of works of art, historical treasures, or other similar assets? *If "Yes,"* *complete Schedule D, Part III*	**8**		X
9	Did the organization report an amount in Part X, line 21; serve as a custodian for amounts not listed in Part X, or provide credit counseling, debt management, credit repair, or debt negotiation services? *If "Yes,"* *complete Schedule D, Part IV*	**9**		X
10	Did the organization, directly or through a related organization, hold assets in temporarily restricted endowments, permanent endowments, or quasi-endowments? *If "Yes," complete Schedule D, Part V*	**10**	X	
11	If the organization's answer to any of the following questions is "Yes," then complete Schedule D, Parts VI, VII, VIII, IX, or X as applicable.			
a	Did the organization report an amount for land, buildings, and equipment in Part X, line 10? *If "Yes," complete Schedule D, Part VI*	**11a**	X	
b	Did the organization report an amount for investments—othersecurities in Part X, line 12 that is 5% or more of its total assets reported in Part X, line 16? *If "Yes," complete Schedule D, Part VII*	**11b**	X	
c	Did the organization report an amount for investments-program related in Part X, line 13 that is 5% or more of its total assets reported in Part X, line 16? *If "Yes," complete Schedule D, Part VIII*	**11c**		X
d	Did the organization report an amount for other assets in Part X, line 15 that is 5% or more of its total assets reported in Part X, line 16? *If "Yes," complete Schedule D, Part IX*	**11d**		X
e	Did the organization report an amount for other liabilities in Part X, line 25? *If "Yes," complete Schedule D, Part X*	**11e**	X	
f	Did the organization's separate or consolidated financial statements for the tax year include a footnote that addresses the organization's liability for uncertain tax positions under FIN 48 (ASC 740)? *If "Yes," complete Schedule D, Part X*	**11f**	X	
12 a	Did the organization obtain separate, independent audited financial statements for the tax year? *If "Yes,"* *complete Schedule D, Parts XI, XII, and XIII*	**12a**	X	
b	Was the organization included in consolidated, independent audited financial statements for the tax year? *If "Yes," and if the organization answered "No" to line 12a, then completing Schedule D, Parts XI, XII, and XIII is optional*	**12b**		X
13	Is the organization a school described in section 170(b)(1)(A)(ii)? *If "Yes," complete Schedule E*	**13**		X
14 a	Did the organization maintain an office, employees, or agents outside of the United States?	**14a**		X
b	Did the organization have aggregate revenues or expenses of more than $10,000 from grantmaking, fundraising, business, investment, and program service activities outside the United States, or aggregate foreign investments valued at $100,000 or more? *If "Yes," complete Schedule F, Parts I and IV*	**14b**		X
15	Did the organization report on Part IX, column (A), line 3, more than $5,000 of grants or assistance to any organization or entity located outside the United States? *If "Yes," complete Schedule F, Parts II and IV*	**15**		X
16	Did the organization report on Part IX, column (A), line 3, more than $5,000 of aggregate grants or assistance to individuals located outside the United States? *If "Yes," complete Schedule F, Parts III and IV*	**16**		X
17	Did the organization report a total of more than $15,000 of expenses for professional fundraising services on Part IX, column (A), lines 6 and 11e? *If "Yes," complete Schedule G, Part I (see instructions)*	**17**	X	
18	Did the organization report more than $15,000 total of fundraising event gross income and contributions on Part VIII, lines 1c and 8a? *If "Yes," complete Schedule G, Part II*	**18**	X	
19	Did the organization report more than $15,000 of gross income from gaming activities on Part VIII, line 9a? *If "Yes," complete Schedule G, Part III*	**19**		X
20 a	Did the organization operate one or more hospital facilities? *If "Yes," complete Schedule H*	**20a**		X
b	If "Yes" to line 20a, did the organization attach a copy of its audited financial statements to this return?	**20b**		

JSA   Form **990** (2011)

1.000

90958W L161 4/3/2012   9:10:34 AM   V 11-4.1

Know More Nonprofits

Form 990 (2011)   Page **4**

Part IV   **Checklist of Required Schedules** *(continued)*

		Yes	No
21	Did the organization report more than $5,000 of grants and other assistance to any government or organization in the United States on Part IX, column (A), line 1? *If "Yes," complete Schedule I, Parts I and II*. **21**		X
22	Did the organization report more than $5,000 of grants and other assistance to individuals in the United States on Part IX, column (A), line 2? *If "Yes," complete Schedule I, Parts I and III*. **22**		X
23	Did the organization answer "Yes" to Part VII, Section A, line 3, 4, or 5 about compensation of the organization's current and former officers, directors, trustees, key employees, and highest compensated employees? *If "Yes," complete Schedule J* **23**	X	
24 a	Did the organization have a tax-exempt bond issue with an outstanding principal amount of more than $100,000 as of the last day of the year, that was issued after December 31, 2002? *If "Yes," answer lines 24b through 24d and complete Schedule K. If "No," go to line 25*. **24a**	X	
b	Did the organization invest any proceeds of tax-exempt bonds beyond a temporary period exception? **24b**		X
c	Did the organization maintain an escrow account other than a refunding escrow at any time during the year to defease any tax-exempt bonds? **24c**		X
d	Did the organization act as an "on behalf of" issuer for bonds outstanding at any time during the year? **24d**		X
25 a	**Section 501(c)(3) and 501(c)(4) organizations.** Did the organization engage in an excess benefit transaction with a disqualified person during the year? *If "Yes," complete Schedule L, Part I* **25a**		X
b	Is the organization aware that it engaged in an excess benefit transaction with a disqualified person in a prior year, and that the transaction has not been reported on any of the organization's prior Forms 990 or 990-EZ? *If "Yes," complete Schedule L, Part I*. **25b**		X
26	Was a loan to or by a current or former officer, director, trustee, key employee, highly compensated employee, or disqualified person outstanding as of the end of the organization's tax year? *If "Yes," complete Schedule L, Part II* . **26**		X
27	Did the organization provide a grant or other assistance to an officer, director, trustee, key employee, substantial contributor or employee thereof, a grant selection committee member, or to a 35% controlled entity or family member of any of these persons? *If "Yes," complete Schedule L, Part III* **27**		X
28	Was the organization a party to a business transaction with one of the following parties (see Schedule L, Part IV instructions for applicable filing thresholds, conditions, and exceptions):		
a	A current or former officer, director, trustee, or key employee? *If "Yes," complete Schedule L, Part IV*. **28a**		X
b	A family member of a current or former officer, director, trustee, or key employee? *If "Yes," complete Schedule L, Part IV*. **28b**		X
c	An entity of which a current or former officer, director, trustee, or key employee (or a family member thereof) was an officer, director, trustee, or direct or indirect owner? *If "Yes," complete Schedule L, Part IV* **28c**	X	
29	Did the organization receive more than $25,000 in non-cash contributions? *If "Yes," complete Schedule M*	**29**	X	
30	Did the organization receive contributions of art, historical treasures, or other similar assets, or qualified conservation contributions? *If "Yes," complete Schedule M* **30**		X
31	Did the organization liquidate, terminate, or dissolve and cease operations? *If "Yes," complete Schedule N, Part I*. **31**		X
32	Did the organization sell, exchange, dispose of, or transfer more than 25% of its net assets? *If "Yes," complete Schedule N, Part II*. **32**		X
33	Did the organization own 100% of an entity disregarded as separate from the organization under Regulations sections 301.7701-2 and 301.7701-3? *If "Yes," complete Schedule R, Part I*. **33**		X
34	Was the organization related to any tax-exempt or taxable entity? *If "Yes," complete Schedule R, Parts II, III, IV, and V, line 1* **34**	X	
35 a	Did the organization have a controlled entity within the meaning of section 512(b)(13)? **35a**		X
b	Did the organization receive any payment from or engage in any transaction with a controlled entity within the meaning of section 512(b)(13)? *If "Yes," complete Schedule R, Part V, line 2* **35b**		X
36	**Section 501(c)(3) organizations.** Did the organization make any transfers to an exempt non-charitable related organization? *If "Yes," complete Schedule R, Part V, line 2*. **36**		X
37	Did the organization conduct more than 5% of its activities through an entity that is not a related organization and that is treated as a partnership for federal income tax purposes? *If "Yes," complete Schedule R, Part VI* **37**		X
38	Did the organization complete Schedule O and provide explanations in Schedule O for Part VI, lines 11 and 19? **Note.** All Form 990 filers are required to complete Schedule O. **38**		X

Form **990** (2011)

| 128 |

EXEMPT ORGANIZATION   12-3456789

Form 990 (2011)   Page **5**

Part V	Statements Regarding Other IRS Filings and Tax Compliance

Check if Schedule O contains a response to any question in this Part V. . . . . ▢

			Yes	No
1a Enter the number reported in Box 3 of Form 1096. Enter -0- if not applicable	**1a**	7		
b Enter the number of Forms W-2G included in line 1a. Enter -0- if not applicable	**1b**	0		
c Did the organization comply with backup withholding rules for reportable payments to vendors and reportable gaming (gambling) winnings to prize winners?.		**1c**	X	
2a Enter the number of employees reported on Form W-3, Transmittal of Wage and Tax Statements, filed for the calendar year ending with or within the year covered by this return .	**2a**	124		
b If at least one is reported on line 2a, did the organization file all required federal employment tax returns?		**2b**	X	
Note. If the sum of lines 1a and 2a is greater than 250, you may be required to e-file (see instructions)				
3a Did the organization have unrelated business gross income of $1,000 or more during the year?		**3a**		X
b If "Yes," has it filed a Form 990-T for this year? If "No," provide an explanation in Schedule O		**3b**		
4a At any time during the calendar year, did the organization have an interest in, or a signature or other authority over, a financial account in a foreign country (such as a bank account, securities account, or other financial account)?		**4a**	X	
b If "Yes," enter the name of the foreign country: ▶ CANADA				
See instructions for filing requirements for Form TD F 90-22.1, Report of Foreign Bank and Financial Accounts.				
5a Was the organization a party to a prohibited tax shelter transaction at any time during the tax year?		**5a**		X
b Did any taxable party notify the organization that it was or is a party to a prohibited tax shelter transaction?		**5b**		X
c If "Yes" to line 5a or 5b, did the organization file Form 8886-T?		**5c**		
6a Does the organization have annual gross receipts that are normally greater than $100,000, and did the organization solicit any contributions that were not tax deductible?		**6a**		X
b If "Yes," did the organization include with every solicitation an express statement that such contributions or gifts were not tax deductible?		**6b**		
7 **Organizations that may receive deductible contributions under section 170(c).**				
a Did the organization receive a payment in excess of $75 made partly as a contribution and partly for goods and services provided to the payor?		**7a**	X	
b If "Yes," did the organization notify the donor of the value of the goods or services provided?		**7b**	X	
c Did the organization sell, exchange, or otherwise dispose of tangible personal property for which it was required to file Form 8282?		**7c**		X
d If "Yes," indicate the number of Forms 8282 filed during the year	**7d**			
e Did the organization receive any funds, directly or indirectly, to pay premiums on a personal benefit contract? . . .		**7e**		X
f Did the organization, during the year, pay premiums, directly or indirectly, on a personal benefit contract? . . .		**7f**		X
g If the organization received a contribution of qualified intellectual property, did the organization file Form 8899 as required? . . .		**7g**		
h If the organization received a contribution of cars, boats, airplanes, or other vehicles, did the organization file a Form 1098-C?		**7h**		
8 **Sponsoring organizations maintaining donor advised funds and section 509(a)(3) supporting organizations.** Did the supporting organization, or a donor advised fund maintained by a sponsoring organization, have excess business holdings at any time during the year?.		**8**		
9 **Sponsoring organizations maintaining donor advised funds.**				
a Did the organization make any taxable distributions under section 4966?		**9a**		
b Did the organization make a distribution to a donor, donor advisor, or related person?		**9b**		
10 **Section 501(c)(7) organizations.** Enter:				
a Initiation fees and capital contributions included on Part VIII, line 12	**10a**			
b Gross receipts, included on Form 990, Part VIII, line 12, for public use of club facilities	**10b**			
11 **Section 501(c)(12) organizations.** Enter:				
a Gross income from members or shareholders	**11a**			
b Gross income from other sources (Do not net amounts due or paid to other sources against amounts due or received from them.)	**11b**			
12a **Section 4947(a)(1) non-exempt charitable trusts.** Is the organization filing Form 990 in lieu of Form 1041?		**12a**		
b If "Yes," enter the amount of tax-exempt interest received or accrued during the year	**12b**			
13 **Section 501(c)(29) qualified nonprofit health insurance issuers.**				
a Is the organization licensed to issue qualified health plans in more than one state?.		**13a**		
Note. See the instructions for additional information the organization must report on Schedule O.				
b Enter the amount of reserves the organization is required to maintain by the states in which the organization is licensed to issue qualified health plans	**13b**			
c Enter the amount of reserves on hand	**13c**			
14a Did the organization receive any payments for indoor tanning services during the tax year?		**14a**		X
b If "Yes," has it filed a Form 720 to report these payments? If "No," provide an explanation in Schedule O		**14b**		

JSA
040 1.000   Form **990** (2011)

90958W L161 4/3/2012   9:10:34 AM   V 11-4.1

EXEMPT ORGANIZATION   12-3456789

Form 990 (2011)   Page **5**

Part V Statements Regarding Other IRS Filings and Tax Compliance

Check if Schedule O contains a response to any question in this Part V . . . . ☐

			Yes	No
1a	Enter the number reported in Box 3 of Form 1096. Enter -0- if not applicable	1a	7		
b	Enter the number of Forms W-2G included in line 1a. Enter -0- if not applicable	1b	0		
c	Did the organization comply with backup withholding rules for reportable payments to vendors and reportable gaming (gambling) winnings to prize winners?.			1c	X	
2a	Enter the number of employees reported on Form W-3, Transmittal of Wage and Tax Statements, filed for the calendar year ending with or within the year covered by this return .	2a	124		
b	If at least one is reported on line 2a, did the organization file all required federal employment tax returns?			2b	X	
	Note. If the sum of lines 1a and 2a is greater than 250, you may be required to *e-file* (see instructions)					
3a	Did the organization have unrelated business gross income of $1,000 or more during the year?			3a		X
b	If "Yes," has it filed a Form 990-T for this year? *If "No," provide an explanation in Schedule O*			3b		
4a	At any time during the calendar year, did the organization have an interest in, or a signature or other authority over a financial account in a foreign country (such as a bank account, securities account, or other financial account)?			4a	X	
b	If "Yes," enter the name of the foreign country: ▶ CANADA					
	See instructions for filing requirements for Form TD F 90-22.1, Report of Foreign Bank and Financial Accounts.					
5a	Was the organization a party to a prohibited tax shelter transaction at any time during the tax year?			5a		X
b	Did any taxable party notify the organization that it was or is a party to a prohibited tax shelter transaction?			5b		X
c	If "Yes" to line 5a or 5b, did the organization file Form 8886-T?			5c		
6a	Does the organization have annual gross receipts that are normally greater than $100,000, and did the organization solicit any contributions that were not tax deductible?			6a		X
b	If "Yes," did the organization include with every solicitation an express statement that such contributions or gifts were not tax deductible?			6b		
7	**Organizations that may receive deductible contributions under section 170(c).**					
a	Did the organization receive a payment in excess of $75 made partly as a contribution and partly for goods and services provided to the payor?			7a	X	
b	If "Yes," did the organization notify the donor of the value of the goods or services provided?			7b	X	
c	Did the organization sell, exchange, or otherwise dispose of tangible personal property for which it was required to file Form 8282?			7c		X
d	If "Yes," indicate the number of Forms 8282 filed during the year	7d				
e	Did the organization receive any funds, directly or indirectly, to pay premiums on a personal benefit contract? . . .			7e		X
f	Did the organization, during the year, pay premiums, directly or indirectly, on a personal benefit contract?			7f		X
g	If the organization received a contribution of qualified intellectual property, did the organization file Form 8899 as required? . . .			7g		
h	If the organization received a contribution of cars, boats, airplanes, or other vehicles, did the organization file a Form 1098-C?			7h		
8	**Sponsoring organizations maintaining donor advised funds and section 509(a)(3) supporting organizations.** Did the supporting organization, or a donor advised fund maintained by a sponsoring organization, have excess business holdings at any time during the year?.			8		
9	**Sponsoring organizations maintaining donor advised funds.**					
a	Did the organization make any taxable distributions under section 4966?			9a		
b	Did the organization make a distribution to a donor, donor advisor, or related person?			9b		
10	**Section 501(c)(7) organizations.** Enter:					
a	Initiation fees and capital contributions included on Part VIII, line 12	10a				
b	Gross receipts, included on Form 990, Part VIII, line 12, for public use of club facilities	10b				
11	**Section 501(c)(12) organizations.** Enter:					
a	Gross income from members or shareholders	11a				
b	Gross income from other sources (Do not net amounts due or paid to other sources against amounts due or received from them.)	11b				
12a	**Section 4947(a)(1) non-exempt charitable trusts.** Is the organization filing Form 990 in lieu of Form 1041?			12a		
b	If "Yes," enter the amount of tax-exempt interest received or accrued during the year	12b				
13	**Section 501(c)(29) qualified nonprofit health insurance issuers.**					
a	Is the organization licensed to issue qualified health plans in more than one state?.			13a		
	Note. See the instructions for additional information the organization must report on Schedule O.					
b	Enter the amount of reserves the organization is required to maintain by the states in which the organization is licensed to issue qualified health plans	13b				
c	Enter the amount of reserves on hand	13c				
14a	Did the organization receive any payments for indoor tanning services during the tax year?			14a		X
b	If "Yes," has it filed a Form 720 to report these payments? *If "No," provide an explanation in Schedule O*			14b		

JSA
040 1.000   Form **990** (2011)

90958W L161 4/3/2012   9:10:34 AM   V 11-4.1

- TIME AUDIT -

Quarterly

	%	Apr-Jun	%	Jul-Sept	%	Oct-Dec	%
Meetings	22%	55	21%	65	31%	55	23%
Administration	36%	102	39%	57	27%	70	29%
Training	7%	10	4%	5	2%	5	2%
Direct Services	23%	55	21%	45	21%	70	29%
Projects	12%	22	8%	35	17%	40	16%
Miscellaneous	1%	15	6%	5	2%		1%
Total		259		212		243	

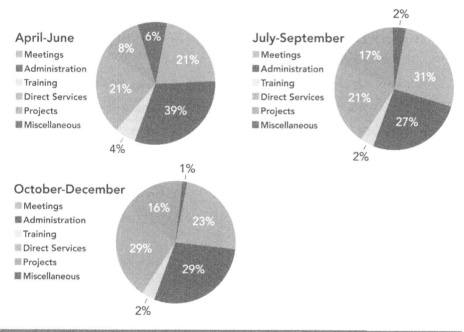

April-June
- Meetings
- Administration
- Training
- Direct Services
- Projects
- Miscellaneous

July-September
- Meetings
- Administration
- Training
- Direct Services
- Projects
- Miscellaneous

October-December
- Meetings
- Administration
- Training
- Direct Services
- Projects
- Miscellaneous

Annual

	2014	%
Meetings	234.50	23%
Administration	327	33%
Training	40	4%
Direct Services	231.50	23%
Projects	129.50	13%
Miscellaneous	24.65	2%
Total	987.15	

2014
- Meetings
- Administration
- Training
- Direct Services
- Projects
- Miscellaneous

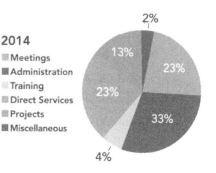

- RESOURCES -

Daron Acemoglu and James A. Robinson, *Why Nations Fail: The Origins of Power, Prosperity, and Poverty* (New York: Crown Publishing, 2012).

Paul Alofs, *Passion Capital: The World's Most Valuable Asset* (Toronto, Ontario: McClelland & Stewart Ltd, 2012).

Edward E. Baptist, *The Half Has Never Been Told: Slavery and the Making of American Capitalism* (New York: Basic Books, 2014).

Sven Beckert, *Empire of Cotton: A Global History* (New York: Random House Inc., 2014).

Douglas A. Blackmon, *Slavery by Another Name: The Re-Enslavement of Black Americans from the Civil War to World War II* (New York: Anchor Books, 2008).

David W. Blight, *Race and Reunion: The Civil War in American History* (The Belknap Press of Harvard University Press, 2001).

Andrew Carnegie, *The Autobiography of Andrew Carnegie* (Filiquarian Publishing, LLC, 2006).

Ta-Nehisi Coates, *Between the World and Me* (New York: Spiegel & Grau, 2015).

Jim Collins, *Good to Great and the Social Sectors: Why Business Thinking Is Not the Answer* (Jim Collins, 2005).

Dalton Conley, *Being Black, Living in the Red: Race, Wealth, and Social Policy in America* (Berkley & Los Angeles, CA: University of California Press, 1999, 2019).

Rev. Dr. Don L. Davis, *Black & Human: Rediscovering King as a Resource for Black Theology and Ethics* (Wichita, KA: TUMI Press, 2000).

Robin Diangelo, *White Fragility: Why It's So Hard for White People to Talk about Racism* (Boston, Massachusetts: Beacon Press Boston, 2018).

Peter F. Drucker, *Managing the Nonprofit Organization: Principles and Practices* (New York: Harper Collins Publisher, 1990).

Robert W. Fairlie and Alicia M. Robb, *Race and Entrepreneurial Success: Black-, Asian, -and White-Owned Businesses in the United States* (MIT Press, 2008).

Henry Louis Gates, Jr. and Donald Yacovone, *The African Americans: Many Rivers to Cross* (US: Smiley Books, 2013).

Malcom Gladwell, *Blink: The Power of Thinking Without Thinking* (New York: Little Brown and Company, 2005).

Malcom Gladwell, *The Story of Success* (New York: Little Brown and Company, 2008).

Eddie S. Glaude Jr., *Democracy in Black: How Race Still Enslaves the American Soul* (New York: Crown Publishing Group, 2016).

Dominique Dubois Gillard, *Rethinking Incarceration: Advocating for Justice that Restores* (Downers Grove, IL: InterVarsity Press, 2018).

Peter Greer and Chris Horst, *The Mission Drift: The Unspoken Crisis Facing Leaders, Charities, and Churches* (Minneapolis, Minnesota: Bethany House Publishers, 2014).

Jason Haber, *The Business of Good: Social Entrepreneurship and the New Bottom Line* (Irvine, CA: Entrepreneur Press, 2016).

Ryan Honeyman, *The B Corp Handbook: How to Use Business as a Force for Good* (San Francisco, CA: Berrett-Koehler Publishers Inc, 2014).

Nancy Isenberg, *White Trash: The 400-Year Untold History of Class in America* (New York: Penguin Books, 2016).

Martin Luther King, Jr. *Where Do We Go from Here: Chaos or Community?* (Boston, MA: Beacon Press, 2010).

Martin Luther King, Jr., *Why We Can't Wait*, reprint (New York: Penguin Group USA Inc., 2005).

Marc J. Lane, *The Mission-Driven Venture: Business Solutions to the World's Most Vexing Social Problems* (Hoboken, New Jersey: John Wiley & Sons, Inc., 2015).

Charles T. Lee, *Good Idea. Now What? How to Move Ideas to Execution* (Hoboken, New Jersey: John Wiley & Sons, Inc., 2012).

Corinda Pitts Marsh, *Holocaust in the Homeland* (Lexington, KY: Createspace, 2014).

John C. Maxwell, *The 360 Leader: Developing Your Influence from Anywhere in the Organization* (Nashville, TN: Thomas Nelson, 2005).

Sowande' M. Mustakeem, *Slavery at Sea: Terror, Sex, and Sickness in the Middle Passage* (Urbana, Chicago, and Springfield, IL: University of Illinois Press, 2016).

Bishop George D. McKinney, *The New Slave Masters* (Eastbourne, England: Life Journey, 2005).

Mike Michalowicz, *The Toilet Paper Entrepreneur: The Tell-It-Like-It-Is Guide to Cleaning Up in Business, Even If You Are at the End of Your Roll* (Boonton, New Jersey: Obsidian Launch LLC, 2008).

Natalie Y. Moore, *The South Side: A Portrait of Chicago and American Segregation* (New York: St. Martin's Press, 2016).

Mark A. Noll, *The Scandal of the Evangelical Mind* (Grand Rapids, Michigan: Wm B. Eerdmans Publishing Co., 1994).

Thomas Piketty, *Capital in the Twenty-First Century* (The Belknap Press of Harvard University Press, 2014).

Soong-Chan Rah: *The Next Evangelicalism: Freeing the Church from Western Cultural Captivity*

(Downers Grove, IL: InterVarsity Press, 2009).

David O. Renz & Associates, *The Jossey-Bass Handbook of Nonprofit Leadership and Management* (San Francisco, CA: Jossey-Bass, 2010).

Eric Ries, *The Lean StartUp: How Today's Entrepreneurs Use Continuous Innovation to Create Radically Successful Businesses* (New York: Crown Publishing Group, 2011).

W. Sherman Rogers, *The African American Entrepreneur: Then & Now* (Santa Barbara, CA: ABC-CLIO, LLC, 2010).

Richard Rothstein, *The Color of Law: A Forgotten History of How Our Government Segregated America* (New York: Live Right Publishing Corporation, 2017).

Michael Shaara, *The Killer Angels: The Classic Novel of the Civil War* (New York & Toronto Canada: The Random House Publishing Group, 2003 & 1998).

Kenneth M. Stampp, *The Peculiar Institution: Slavery in the Ante-Bellum South* (New York: Vintage Books, 1956).

Hugh Thomas, *The Slave Trade* (New York: Simon and Schuster, 1997).

Jemar Tisby, *The Color of Compromise* (Grand Rapids, Michigan: Zondervan, 2019).

Larry Tye, *Rising from the Rails: Pullman Porters and the Making of the Black Middle Class* (New York: Henry Holt & Company, 2004).

Isabel Wilkerson, *The Warmth of Other Suns: The Epic Story of America's Great Migration* (New York: Random House, 2010).

- ADDITIONAL SOURCES -

1   Jenkins, L. Brian. *Starting up Now: 24 Steps to Launch Your Own Business.* StartingUp Business Solutions, 2011.

2   *"Education & Training Services Industry Profile."* First Research, Dunn and Bradstreet, 2 Jan. 2019, www.firstresearch.com/industry-research/Education-and-Training-Services html

3   Andrew Carnegie, *The Autobiography of Andrew Carnegie* (Filiquarian Publishing, LLC 2006).

4   *Wealth by Andrew Carnegie.* Edited by Robert Bannister, Swarthmore College, 1995, www swarthmore.edu/SocSci/rbannis1/AIH19th/Carnegie.html

5   McKeever, B. S., & Perrijohn, S. L. (2014, October). *The Nonprofit Sector in Brief 201 - Public Charities, Giving, and Volunteering.* Retrieved from https://www.urban.org/site default/files/publication/33711/413277-The-Nonprofit-Sector-in-Brief--.PDF

6   Grimm, B. J., & Grimm, M. (2016). The Socio-economic Contribution of Religion to American Society: An Empirical Analysis. Retrieved from http://www.religjournal.com/

7   Ibid., 27

8   Ibid., 4

9   Smith, G. A., & Cooperman, A. (2016, September 14). *The factors driving the growth of religious 'nones' in the U.S.* Retrieved from https://www.pewresearch.org/fact-tank/2016/09/14/the-factors-driving-the-growth-of-religious-nones-in-the-u-s/

10 Blight, David. *"1. Introductions: Why Does the Civil War Era Have a Hold on American Historical."* YouTube, YaleCourses, 21 Nov. 2008, www.youtube.com/watch?v=QXXp1bHd6gI

11 Coates, Ta-Nehisi. *"What Cotton Hath Wrought."* The Atlantic, Atlantic Media Company, 30 July 2010, www.theatlantic.com/personal/archive/2010/07/what-cotton-hath-wrought/60666/

12 *"List of Landmark African-American Legislation."* Wikipedia, Wikimedia Foundation, 4 Apr. 2019, en.wikipedia.org/wiki/List_of_landmark_African-American_legislation

13 Thomas, Hugh. *The Slave Trade: the Story of the Atlantic Slave Trade, 1440-1870.* Simon & Schuster, 1999.

14 *"U.S. Constitution - Amendment 14 - The U.S. Constitution Online."* Amendment 14 - The U.S. Constitution Online - USConstitution.net, www.usconstitution.net/xconst_Am14.html

15 Martin Luther King, Jr. *Where Do We Go from Here: Chaos or Community?* (Boston, MA: Beacon Press, 2010).

16 *"Luke 19, New International Version (NIV) | The Bible App."* Holy Bible, YouVersion, 1996, www.bible.com/bible/111/LUK.19.NIV

17 Dalton Conley, *Being Black, Living in the Red: Race, Wealth, and Social Policy in America* (Berkley & Los Angeles, CA: University of California Press, 1999, 2019).

18 "Brown v. Board of Education (1954)." *Our Documents - Brown v. Board of Education (1954)*, www.ourdocuments.gov/doc.php?flash=false&doc=87#

19 "Plessy v. Ferguson (1896)." *Our Documents - Plessy v. Ferguson (1896)*, www.ourdocuments.gov/doc.php?flash=false&doc=52

20 Amerikaner, Ary. *"Funding Gaps 2018."* The Education Trust, edtrust.org/resource/funding-gaps-2018/

21 MyFootage001. *"Dr. King - Housing March in Gage Park Chicago, 1966."* YouTube, 18 Oct. 2007, www.youtube.com/watch?v=r_pjbnMXM1o

22 *The Bible: New International Version.* International Bible Society, 1984.

24 Blake, Erick S, et al. *"THE DEADLIEST, COSTLIEST, AND MOST INTENSE UNITED STATES TROPICAL CYCLONES FROM 1851 TO 2010 (AND OTHER FREQUENTLY REQUESTED HURRICANE FACTS)."* Most Extreme Tropical Cyclones, National Hurricane Center, 2011, www.nhc.noaa.gov/dcmi.shtml

25 Jenkins, L. Brian. *Starting up Now: 24 Steps to Launch Your Own Business.* StartingUp Business Solutions, 2011.

26 Jenkins, L. Brian. *Starting up Now Facilitator Guide.* StartingUp Business Solutions, 2011.

27 Olsen, Erik. "SERE Training Develops Leaders for Complex Environment." Www.army. mil, 21 Nov. 2014, www.army.mil/article/138765/SERE_training_develops_leaders_for_complex_environment/

28 Jim Collins, *Good to Great and the Social Sectors: Why Business Thinking Is Not the Answer* (Jim Collins, 2005), 41-64.

29 Plantation Biographies, haygenealogy.com/hay/patriots/civilwar/plantationbios.html.

30 Jane Brazy, Martha. "Stephen Duncan." Mississippi Encyclopedia, Center for Study of Southern Culture, 19 Apr. 2018, mississippiencyclopedia.org/entries/stephen-duncan/.

31 "Inflation Rate between 1860-2019 | Inflation Calculator." $0 In 1860 → 2019 | Inflation Calculator, www.in2013dollars.com/us/inflation/1860?amount=100.

32 Revolvy, LLC. "Connect with People Who Have Interests Similar to Your Own on Revolvy. com." Trending Topics, www.revolvy.com/.

- RECOMMENDED READING -

Slavery and the Making of America
– PBS video series

Slavery at Sea: Terror, Sex, and Sickness in the Middle Passage
– Sowande M. Mustakeem

The Half Has Never Been Told: Slavery and the Making of American Capitalism – Edward E. Baptist

The African Americans: Many Rivers to Cross
– PBS miniseries

The New Jim Crow
– Michelle Alexander

White Fragility
– Robin DiAngelo

A Testament of Hope: The Essential Writings and Speeches
– Martin Luther King Jr.

Our Kind of People
– Lawrence Otis Graham

Becoming
– Michelle Obama

Sundown Towns
– James W. Loewen

The West Point Way of Leadership
–Col. Larry R. Donnithorne (Ret.)

Beloved
–Toni Morrison

Of Mules and Men
– Zora Neale Hurston

Their Eyes Were Watching God
– Zora Neale Hurston

- ACKNOWLEDGMENTS -

When something of substance is created, it is usually the work of a team, not just an individual. I'd like to personally thank Randi Craigen, who helped edit multiple versions of *Know More* and reminded me to, "Get It Done." Randi's ability as a developmental editor is on full display and makes *Know More* a better read. I want to thank Kathyjo "KJ" Varco, whose keen sense of design and concept has resulted in the finished product of *Know More*. I appreciate KJ's ability to listen and hear me as I draft ideas. My long-term advisor, Stephen Fraser, who does not always tell me what I want to hear but tells me what I need to know. I appreciate your friendship and trust. I want to thank Dr. Hazel King, who hired me in 2000 and whose business model indirectly forced me to live out the "70/30 Principle." Thank you for believing that I had value to offer the youth and adults of Chicago. Lastly, to Mark Soderquist, whose friendship and financial commitment to an upstart nonprofit 20-years ago helped fuel the idea that the urban context needs businesses, not just nonprofits, to improve the lives of communities often in economic chaos.

Sincerely,
L. Brian Jenkins

SUN STARTINGUP NOW

StartingUp Now is a print and cloud based-entrepreneurial business development curriculum for new entrepreneurs seeking simple, solution-oriented tools to establish and launch a business.

- **StartingUp Now: 24 Steps to Launch Your Own Business** simplifies necessary business aspects, using real-life scenarios to provide critical guidance through each aspect of business development.

  Book Price: $19.95

- **StartingUp Now: Facilitator Guide** teaches instructors how to use StartingUp Now as a business planning resource for startups, first and secondary school systems, colleges, prisons, churches and community organizations.

  Book Price: $29.95

- **StartingUp Now: Skillcenter,** provides secure real-time access to StartingUp Now: 24 Steps Book, Business Plan Template, Financial Tools Suite, SUN Talks Video Series & Learning Guides and an opportunity to create, collaborate and connect with like-minded entrepreneurs from any device. iTunes Google Play

  Basic Membership: Free
  Pro Membership: Youth $95/year | Adult $195.00/year

- **SUNTalks** 5-7 minute video segments led by entrepreneurs and business leaders for each chapter in StartingUp Now: 24 Steps. Each SUN Talk has an accompanying hard copy Learning Guide to help capture the content and guides to apply the content to businesses.

  Included with Skillcenter Pro Membership

KNOW MORE
NONPROFITS

**MOVING FROM DEPENDENCY
TO SUSTAINABILITY**

WORKSHOP

Take *Know More Nonprofits* to the next level with an in-depth workshop on sustainability strategies for nonprofit leaders, including:

- How Wealth Works in the Nonprofit Industry
- Sustainability Attracts Donors, Not Dependency
- Strategy Builders: Gleaning & Digesting 990s
- Steps to Launching Your Own Sustainability Model
- Private Funding vs. Tax Payer Dollars

DREAMIT. PLANIT. LAUNCHIT.
For more information, call 855-478-2786 or visit startingupnow.com

STARTING**UP NOW**
&
KNOW MORE
NONPROFITS

DUO WORKSHOPS

Get exposed to practical tools and resources for entrepreneurship training and business development. Explore the challenges facing nonprofit leaders, as well as best practices for long-term business sustainability, in this value-packed workshop with *StartingUp Now* and *Know More Nonprofits*. Find out more at StartingUp Now.com

- ABOUT THE AUTHOR -

L. Brian Jenkins is the founder and president of Entrenuity, NFP and StartingUp Business Solutions, Inc. and founding partner of Renew Pavement Solutions, Inc. His efforts have successfully provided entrepreneurship education training and small business development for more than 20 years in Chicago, nationally and abroad. He is responsible for the training of thousands of urban youth and leaders in the fundamentals of entrepreneurship, financial literacy, and character/integrity-based business operations.

Brian has served as adjunct faculty at Moody Bible Institute; Illinois State University's College of Business; The Urban Ministry Institute in Wichita, KS; North Park University's School of Adult Learning; and Wheaton College's Center for Urban Engagement, focusing on entrepreneurship education. He is a graduate of the University of Iowa with dual Bachelor of Arts degrees in English and Religion; additionally, he earned his Master of Arts in Theology from Wheaton College Graduate School. Brian is the author of *StartingUp Now 24 Steps to Launch Your Own Business* and *Know More Nonprofits: Moving From Dependency to Sustainability.*

Brian has been married for 25 years to Dr. Jenai Jenkins, and they've been blessed with three children—Bria (23), Braxton (20), and Brooke (12). Brian and his family live in the Austin community on Chicago's west side.

Made in the USA
Monee, IL
24 July 2021